CONSENT

Praise for *Consent*

"Lucid and nuanced . . . [*Consent*] will speak to trauma survivors everywhere."
—*Los Angeles Review of Books*

"*Consent* is that elegantly laid trap, a memoir that asks sharp questions about desire, literature, and a culture that fetishizes female youth and inexperience over female art."
—*The Paris Review*

"*Consent* [is] rapier-sharp, written with restraint, elegance, and brevity."
—*The Times* (London)

"[*Consent*] has something steely in its heart, and it departs from the typical American memoir of childhood abuse in exhilarating ways."
—Slate

"*Consent* is a Molotov cocktail, flung at the face of the French establishment, a work of dazzling, highly controlled fury. . . . By every conceivable metric, her book is a triumph."
—*New York Times*

"A piercing memoir about the sexually abusive relationship she endured at age 14 with a 50-year-old writer . . . This chilling account will linger with readers long after the last page is turned."
—*Publishers Weekly*

"A fierce account from a woman hoping to wrest her story back. Recommended Reading."
—*Library Journal*

"Springora's lucid account is a commanding discussion of sexual abuse and victimization, and a powerful act of reclamation."
—*Booklist*

"A chilling story of child abuse and the sophisticated Parisians who looked the other way . . . [Springora] is an elegant and perceptive writer."
—*Kirkus Reviews*

"One of the belated truths that emerges from [*Consent*] is that Springora is a writer. . . . Her sentences gleam like metal; each chapter snaps shut with the clean brutality of a latch."
—*The New Yorker*

"In elegant, focused prose, fluidly translated by Natasha Lehrer . . . With admirable restraint—another author might have been tempted to veer off into disquisitions on De Sade, Balthus, or Nabokov—Springora describes how Matzneff expertly manipulated her into believing she had as much agency and power as he did."
—*The Guardian*

"Springora's style is incisive and she keeps readers hooked with short chapters depicting a post-1968 libertarian establishment that lets her down."
—*Financial Times*

"Even if he is acquitted, Springora has managed to exact some revenge by capturing G., and all of his terrible behavior, forever in these erudite, incriminating pages."
—New York Journal of Books

"[*Consent*] is really about power; who we give it to, and where it should be curtailed. It is also about correcting an imbalance."
—*The Sunday Times* (London)

CONSENT

A Memoir

VANESSA SPRINGORA

Translated from the French by Natasha Lehrer

HARPERVIA

An Imprint of HarperCollins*Publishers*

HarperCollins books may be purchased for educational, business, or sales promotional use. For information, please email the Special Markets Department at SPsales@harpercollins.com.

Originally published as *Le Consentement* in France in 2020 by Editions Grasset & Fasquelle.

FIRST HARPERCOLLINS PAPERBACK EDITION PUBLISHED IN 2022

Designed by SBI Book Arts, LLC

Library of Congress Cataloging-in-Publication Data is available upon request.

ISBN 978-0-06-304790-7

22 23 24 25 26 LSC 10 9 8 7 6 5 4 3 2 1

For Benjamin and Raoul

Prologue

Fairy tales are an age-old source of wisdom. Why else have they stood the test of time so well? Cinderella ought to do all she can to leave the ball before midnight; Red Riding Hood ought to be wary of the wolf and his cajoling voice; Sleeping Beauty ought to keep her finger far from the irresistible temptation of the spindle; Snow White ought to evade the hunters, and nothing on earth should tempt her to take a bite from the oh-so-red, mouthwatering apple that fate holds out to her.

So many warnings that every child would be wise to follow to the letter.

One of my very first books was the collected stories of the Brothers Grimm. I read it so often, eventually it began to fall apart—the stitches beneath the thick cardboard cover grew frayed, and then the pages began to peel away one by one. I was inconsolable at the loss. Even though these wonderful stories spoke to me of timeless legends, books themselves were earthly objects, destined for the scrap heap.

Before I could even read or write, I used to make books with whatever I had at hand: newspapers, magazines, cardboard, sticky tape, string. As solid as possible. First the object. My interest in the content came later.

Today, I view books with suspicion. A glass wall has been erected between them and me. I know they can be poison. I recognize the toxic load they can contain.

For many years I paced around my cage, my dreams filled with murder and revenge. Until the day when the solution finally presented itself to me, like something that was completely obvious: Why not ensnare the hunter in his own trap, ambush him within the pages of a book?

Part One

THE CHILD

Our wisdom begins where the author's ends; we would like him to give us answers, when all he can do is give us desires.

—Marcel Proust, *On Reading*

AT THE THRESHOLD OF LIFE, UNBLEMISHED BY EXPERIENCE, my name is V., and, at the grand old age of five, I am waiting for love.

Fathers are meant to be their daughters' protectors. Mine is no more than a current of air. More than his physical presence, I can summon up the scent of vetiver filling the bathroom in the morning; masculine belongings dotted the apartment: a tie, wristwatch, shirt, Dupont lighter; a way of holding his cigarette between the index and middle fingers, quite far from the filter; a perpetually ironic way of speaking, so I never know if he's joking or not. He leaves early and comes home late. He's a busy man. Terribly elegant too. His professional activities change too rapidly for me to grasp what they are. At school, whenever I am asked what he does, I don't know what to call him, but the evidence suggests—since he is more drawn to the outside world than to family life—that he is someone important. At least that's what I imagine. His suits are always impeccable.

My mother had me young, when she was twenty. She's beautiful, with Scandinavian blond hair, an enchanting face, light blue eyes, a graceful, shapely figure, and a lovely voice. My worship of her has no limits; she is my sun, the source of my happiness.

My parents are so well matched, my grandmother often says, a nod to their cinematic good looks. We ought to have been happy, yet my memories of our life together, in the apartment where I briefly experienced the illusion of a family unit, are like a bad dream.

At night, buried beneath the covers, I hear my father yelling, calling my mother a "whore" or a "slut," but I don't understand why. At the slightest provocation—a detail, a glance, a single "inappropriate" word—he explodes with jealousy. Out of the blue, the walls begin to shake, crockery flies, doors slam. An obsessive perfectionist, he cannot stand anything being moved without his permission. One day, he almost strangles my mother when she spills a glass of wine on a white tablecloth he's just given her. The frequency of such scenes accelerates. He is a machine propelled by an insane momentum that no one can stop. My parents spend hours flinging bitter insults at each other. Until late one evening when my mother takes refuge in my bedroom, weeping in silence as she snuggles up against me in my little cot bed, before going back to sleep alone in the marital bed. The next night too my father sleeps on the sofa in the living room.

My mother has exhausted all her defensive artillery against my father's uncontrolled bouts of anger and childish tantrums. There is no remedy for dealing with the madness of this man people describe as "temperamental." Their marriage is an ongoing battle, a carnage whose origins everyone has forgotten. The conflict will soon be settled unilaterally. It's a matter of weeks now.

Yet they must have loved each other once. At the end of an interminable corridor, screened by a bedroom door, their sexuality is like a monster crouching just beyond my field of vision: omnipresent (my father's outbursts of jealousy are the daily evidence) but completely covert (I have no memory of the slightest embrace, the slightest kiss, the tiniest gesture of affection between my parents).

What I am trying to do more than anything, without realizing it, is to get to the bottom of the mystery that brings two people together behind a closed bedroom door, what is woven between them there. Like a fairy tale in which the supernatural suddenly bursts into the real, sex—in my imagination a magical process through which babies are miraculously born—can, without any warning, make a sudden and unexpected appearance in real life, in often mystifying forms. Whether brought about intentionally or accidentally, any encounter with this unfathomable force triggers in the child that I am an irresistible, horrified curiosity.

Sometimes, in the middle of the night, I go to my parents' bedroom and stand in the doorway crying, complaining of stomach pain, or a headache, presumably with the unconscious intention of interrupting their lovemaking. I find them with the sheets pulled up to their chins, looking foolish and strangely guilty. Of the image that precedes this, their bodies entwined, I don't recall the faintest trace. It's as if it's been expunged from my memory.

One day my parents were called in by the head teacher of my elementary school. My father didn't come. It was my mother who had to listen, with deep concern, to the report of my diurnal life.

"Your daughter's been falling asleep in class, it's like she's not sleeping at night. I've had to set up a camp bed at the back of the classroom. What's going on? She's mentioned violent nocturnal fights between you and her father. Oh, and one of the lunch ladies told me that V. keeps going to the boys' bathroom at recreation. I asked V. what she does there. She told me, as if it was the most natural thing in the world: 'I'm helping David pee straight. I hold his weenie for him.' David's just been circumcised, and he does seem to have some kind of problem with his . . . aim. I assure you that at the age of five there's nothing unusual about these kinds of games. I just wanted to keep you informed."

One day my mother made an irrevocable decision. Taking advantage of the fact that I was away at camp, a trip she had organized as part of her covert plan to move out, she left my father, definitively. It was the summer before first grade. In the evenings, one of the camp counselors sat down on the edge of my bed and read me letters from my mother, describing our new apartment, my new bedroom, my new school, the new neighborhood, basically the new layout of our new life, once I returned to Paris. From the depths of the countryside where I'd been dispatched, surrounded by the cries of children gone feral in the absence of their parents, it all seemed very abstract. The counselor's eyes grew moist and her voice cracked as she read aloud my mother's letters, filled with fake cheer. After this evening ritual I was sometimes found, in the middle of the night, sleepwalking, crawling backward down the staircase to get to the front door.

organized as part of her covert plan to move out, she left my father definitively. It was the summer before first grade. In the evenings, one of the camp counselors sat down on the edge of my bed and read me letters from my mother, describing our new apartment, my new bedroom, my new school, the new neighborhood. Basically the new layout of our new life once I returned to Paris from the depths of the countryside where I'd been dispatched. Surrounded by the cries of children concerned in the absence of their parents, it all seemed very abstract. The counselor's eyes grew moist and her voice cracked as she read aloud my mother's letters, filled with false cheer. After this evening ritual, I was sometimes found, in the middle of the night, sleepwalking, crawling backward down the staircase to get to the front door.

NOW THAT WE WERE FREE OF THE DOMESTIC TYRANT, our life took an exhilarating turn. We were living in an attic apartment made up of a series of former maids' rooms. I could hardly stand up in my bedroom, and there were secret hiding places everywhere.

I was six years old. A studious little girl, bright and hard-working, obedient and well behaved, and vaguely melancholy, as is often the case with the children of divorced parents. I wasn't secretly rebellious in any way; I went out of my way to avoid committing the slightest misdemeanor. A good little soldier, my principal ambition consisted of bringing home a glowing report card for my mother, whom I still loved more than anything.

In the evenings, she'd play Chopin on the piano into the small hours. Or, with the volume on the hi-fi turned up as high as it would go, we'd dance late into the night; the neighbors, furious, would bang on the walls and yell because the music was too loud, but we didn't care. At the weekend, my mother loved to luxuriate in the bath; she was magnificent, with a Kir Royale in one hand, a John Player Special in the other, an ashtray balanced on the edge of the tub, vermilion fingernails contrasting with her milky skin and platinum blond hair.

The housework could wait.

My father soon managed to wriggle out of paying her alimony. Things were tight at the end of the month. In spite of the regular parties in our apartment, and her—always fleeting—love affairs, my mother turned out to be more solitary than I realized. When I asked her one day about the significance of one of her lovers in her life, she said, "There's no question of me imposing him on you, or replacing your father." She and I were inseparable. No man would ever again be allowed to intrude on our relationship.

At my new school I became best friends with another little girl, called Asia. We learned to read and write together and explored the neighborhood, a charming village with café terraces at every corner. What we shared above all was an unusual freedom. Unlike most of our classmates, we had no one to keep an eye on us at home; there was no money for babysitters, even in the evening. It wasn't worth it. Our mothers completely trusted us. We never misbehaved.

Once, when I was seven, my father invited me to stay over at his apartment. An exceptional occurrence, which was never to be repeated. Since my mother and I had moved out, my old bedroom had been turned into a study.

I went to sleep on the sofa. I woke up at dawn, in this place where I now felt like a stranger. Idly, I inspected his library, which was classified and displayed with meticulous care. I took down two or three books at random, then carefully replaced them. I lingered on a miniature copy of the Koran in Arabic, stroked its tiny red leather cover, tried to decipher its incomprehensible characters. It wasn't a toy, of course, but it did look like one. And what else was I supposed to play with, when there wasn't a single game in the whole place?

An hour later my father got up and came into the living room. The first thing he did was survey the entire space, his gaze alighting on the bookcases. He crouched down on his knees to inspect each shelf. His behavior was a bit deranged. And then, with the obsessive diligence of a tax inspector, he declared triumphantly: "You touched this book, and this one, and this one!" His thundering voice rang across the room. I didn't understand. What could be wrong with touching a book?

What was so horrifying was that he was right, in all three cases. Luckily I wasn't tall enough to reach the top shelf, upon which his eyes lingered longest, and from where his gaze returned to me with a mysterious sigh of relief.

What would he say if he knew that the previous evening, when I'd gone to find something in a cupboard, I'd come face-to-face with a life-size, naked woman, all in latex, with orifices forming horrible hollows and folds where her mouth and sex were, a mocking smile, dead eyes that fastened onto mine, squeezed between a vacuum cleaner and a broom? An image straight from hell, repressed as quickly as the cupboard door was pushed shut.

After school, Asia and I often took the most roundabout way home, to delay the moment we had to say goodbye. At an intersection with two streets there was a little esplanade, at the bottom of a flight of steps, where teenagers gathered to roller-skate or skateboard or smoke cigarettes in little groups. We turned the stone steps into our observation post, where we'd sit and admire the skate tricks that the gangly, show-off boys performed.

One Wednesday afternoon we took our own roller skates there. We started off hesitant and clumsy. The boys teased us a bit, then forgot about us. Intoxicated by speed and the fear that we wouldn't be able to brake in time, we stopped thinking about anything but the joy of gliding. It was winter, and it began to grow dark early. We were getting ready to go, we still had our skates on our feet and our shoes in our hands, our cheeks were on fire, we were out of breath but euphoric.

Out of nowhere a man appeared, wrapped in a big overcoat. He stood in front of us and, with a wide movement of his arms that made him look like an albatross, drew open the flaps of his coat, leaving us speechless before the grotesque sight of his swollen penis extending through the open zipper of his trousers.

Caught between complete panic and hysterical laughter, Asia leapt up, and I followed her, but we both fell flat on our faces, thrown off balance by the skates we'd forgotten we were still wearing. By the time we stood up, the man had disappeared, like a ghost.

My father made a few more brief appearances in my life. On his return from some trip to the other side of the world, he popped over to our apartment to wish me a happy eighth birthday. He arrived with a gift I hadn't dared hope for: the convertible Barbie camper van that all little girls my age dreamed of. I threw myself with gratitude into his arms and spent the next hour unpacking it with the conscientiousness of a collector, thrilled with its banana-yellow exterior and fuchsia-pink interior. It came with over a dozen accessories, a sliding roof, a fold-down kitchen, a deck chair, and a double bed.

A double bed? Calamity! My favorite doll was single, and no matter how much she might stretch out her long legs on her folding chair, exclaiming what a gorgeous day it was, she was going to be crushingly bored. Camping on your own is no fun. Suddenly I remembered a redundant male specimen I'd long ago put away in a drawer, a redheaded Ken with a square jaw, a kind of swaggering lumberjack in a checkered shirt, with whom Barbie would surely feel safe when she was camping in the wild.

It was nighttime. Time for bed. I placed Ken and his lady love side by side on the bed, but it was too hot. I had to take off their clothes first, so they were more comfortable, given the heat wave. Barbie and Ken had no body hair, no genitals, no nipples, it was very odd, but their perfect proportions compensated for this slight defect. I pulled the blanket over their smooth, gleaming bodies and left the roof open to the starry night sky.

My father got up from his chair to leave. He straddled the camper van as I was busily putting everything back in the miniature picnic basket, and then he kneeled down to peer under the awning. A teasing smile warped his face as he pronounced the obscene words.

"Fucking, are they?"

Now it was my cheeks, my forehead, my hands that were fuchsia pink. Some people would never understand the first thing about love.

At the time my mother was working for a small publishing company whose offices occupied the ground floor of our building, three streets from my school. When I didn't go home with Asia, I liked to have my after-school snack in one of the secret corners of this lair, which brimmed with a great jumble of staplers, rolls of tape, reams of paper, Post-its, paper clips, and all kinds of colored pens. A veritable Ali Baba's cave. And then there were the books, hundreds of them, piled up any which way on the rickety old shelves, packed into boxes, gathering dust in the windows, photographed and turned into posters to hang on the walls. My playground was the kingdom of books.

The atmosphere in the courtyard at the end of the day was always merry, especially as the days grew longer. The gardienne, the building's caretaker, would bring out a bottle of champagne from her lodge, set up garden tables and chairs, and an assortment of writers and journalists would hang out there until night fell. All these beautiful people, so cultivated, brilliant, spiritual, and sometimes even famous. It was a marvelous, charmed world. Other professions, those of my friends' parents, of our neighbors, seemed dull and routine in comparison.

One day I too was going to write books.

AFTER MY PARENTS' SEPARATION, I SAW LESS AND LESS OF my father. As a rule, we would meet at dinnertime in very expensive restaurants, including one particular Moroccan establishment decorated with questionable taste, where a voluptuous woman in a risqué costume would suddenly appear at the end of the meal to perform a belly dance a few centimeters away from us. Then came the moment that always filled me with horrified embarrassment: with a look that mingled pride and lust, my father would slip a banknote into the elastic of the beautiful Scheherazade's panties or brassiere. I don't think he even noticed how, as the elastic of her sequined undergarments snapped, I tried to disappear into thin air.

The belly dance was the best-case scenario—in other words, it meant that he had at least bothered to show up. Two times out of three I would sit on a banquette in some prohibitively expensive restaurant waiting for Monsieur to deign to appear. One time a waiter came over and told me, "Your papa called, he is going to be half an hour late." Throwing me a wink from the back of the restaurant, he made me a *sirop à l'eau*. An hour later my father still hadn't shown up. The waiter, perturbed, brought me a third glass of grenadine. Even as he tried to coax a smile from me, I heard him muttering: "How miserable is that! Making the poor kid wait like that, at ten o'clock at night!" And this time it was the waiter who slipped me a banknote, to pay for the taxi to take me home to my mother, who was, obviously, furious at my father, who had waited until the last minute to let her know that, unfortunately, something had come up.

Then came the predictable day when, presumably encouraged by some new girlfriend who also found me a nuisance, he simply stopped showing up at all. It was around this time that I began to develop a particular affection for café waiters, with whom, ever since I was a little girl, I've always felt like part of the family.

SOME CHILDREN SPEND THEIR DAYS CLIMBING TREES. I spent mine in books. This was how I drowned the inconsolable sorrow in which my father's abandonment had left me. Romance and passion filled my imagination. I was far too young for the novels I read, and I understood little of them except that love makes you suffer. Why would anyone want to be destroyed so prematurely?

I finally had a brief glimpse of adult sex one winter's night when I was about nine years old. My mother and I were on vacation in a small family-run hotel in the mountains. Friends of ours were in the room next door. We had a large L-shaped room, and I was sleeping on a cot in the area around the corner, behind a thin dividing wall. After a few days my mother's lover joined us, unbeknown to his wife. He was handsome, artistic, smelled of pipe tobacco, and wore old-fashioned vests and bow ties. He took no interest in me whatsoever. He was frequently irritated to find me doing headstands in front of the television on Wednesday afternoons, when he had managed to escape the attention of his employees so he could spend an hour or two with my mother in her bedroom at the back of our apartment. One day he said to her, "Your daughter is completely wasting her life. You ought to sign her up for activities instead of letting her destroy her brain cells watching garbage all afternoon!"

He arrived in the late afternoon. I was used to him turning up unexpectedly and no longer resented it, but he wasn't the kind of man I could imagine on skis. After dinner I went to bed, leaving the adults to their perplexing conversations. As was my habit, I read a few pages of my book before I fell asleep, my exhausted muscles suddenly lighter than snowflakes, floating, swaying once more down the pristine slopes as sleep carried me off.

I was awoken by the sound of sighing, the friction of bodies and sheets, whispers; I could make out my mother's voice and, with mounting horror, the more peremptory intonation of the man with the moustache. "Turn over" was the only fragment that my ears, suddenly exquisitely keen, managed to distinguish.

I could have put my hands over my ears, or indicated with a light cough that I was awake. But I lay there, petrified, the whole time their lovemaking lasted, trying to slow the rhythm of my breathing and praying that my heartbeat couldn't be heard from the other end of the room, plunged into ominous shadow.

The following summer I spent the vacation in a house in Brittany belonging to a classmate who was to become my best friend. His cousin, a girl a little older than the two of us, joined us for a few days. We slept in a room furnished with bunkbeds, a playhouse, and lots of secret hiding places. No sooner had the adults left the room after one last goodnight kiss, hardly had the bedroom door closed, when, beneath our tents fashioned out of old plaid blankets, our guilty games—though still relatively chaste—would begin. We had a collection of accessories that seemed to us incredibly erotic: feathers, scraps of fabric, velvet and satin torn from old dolls, Venetian masks, silken cords. One of us would be designated the consenting prisoner, while the other two would set about stroking the powerless victim, who was usually blindfolded and handcuffed, nightgown lifted or pajama bottoms lowered, with various objects that we kept hidden under the mattress during the day. We thrilled at these delicious caresses, and sometimes even furtively placed our lips, screened by a piece of fabric, on a nipple or a smooth pubic mound.

We didn't feel at all embarrassed in the morning; the memory of our nocturnal diversions faded away while we slept. The next day we carried on bickering just as always, playing out in the countryside with the same innocence. After we watched the film *Jeux interdits* at the Cinéclub, constructing cemeteries for animals—moles, birds, and insects—became our most absorbing activity. Eros and Thanatos, always.

Julien and I were in the same class, and our games went on for several years, at his house or mine. During the day, we fought like cats and dogs, brother and sister. In the evening, in the darkness of the bedroom, on our little mattresses laid on the floor, we came together like magnets, as if under a magic spell that transformed us into insatiable, lustful beings.

At night, our bodies were drawn to each other as we sought a pleasure that was never satisfied, but the quest itself was enough to make us keep blindly reaching out with the same gestures. What began as clumsy and furtive became, as time went on, increasingly focused. We became masters of the art of contortion, and when it came to devising this new gymnastics, our imagination had no limits. We never reached the paroxysm that we intuitively sought—our knowledge of our bodies was too limited—but we would remain on the cusp of pleasure for long minutes, exquisitely attentive to the effect of our touch on the other, each filled with confused desire, the fear of a tipping point that never came.

Sixth grade signaled the end of our insouciance. One day a red viscous liquid trickled down between my thighs. My mother said to me, "Now you are a woman!" Since my father had fallen off the radar, I had begun desperately trying to attract men's attention. It was a waste of effort. I was completely unattractive; I lacked the slightest physical allure. Not like Asia, who was so pretty, the boys whistled whenever we approached.

Julien and I had both just turned twelve. In the evening, before we moved on to more daring games, we sometimes embraced languorously, but our intimacy never took on the contours of love. There was not the slightest feeling of tenderness between us; we showed no affection to each other during daylight hours. We never held hands, which seemed more daunting than all the things we did at night in our goose-feather alcove. We were anything but "betrothed" as our parents liked to say.

In school, Julien began keeping his distance. Sometimes one of us would go over to see the other, though we might have ignored each other for weeks before that. Julien would tell me about some girl he was in love with. I would listen without letting him see how upset I was. No one liked me. I was too tall, too flat-chested, my hair hung all over my face; one day in the schoolyard a boy even told me I looked like a toad. Asia moved away. Like every girl my age, I bought a notebook and began keeping a journal. As adolescence laid its awkward hands on me, I felt it only as an all-consuming solitude.

To top it all off, the little publishing house on the ground floor of our building went out of business. To make ends meet, my mother took a freelance job proofreading travel guides from home. She spent long hours poring over pages by the kilometer. We had to be careful with money now. Turn out the lights, avoid waste. There were fewer parties; friends rarely came over anymore to play the piano and belt out songs at the top of their voices; my beautiful mother grew dull, withdrew from the world, began drinking too much and spending hours in front of the television. She put on weight, let herself go. She was in such a bad way, she couldn't see that her single life was as much of a burden for me as it was for her.

A father, conspicuous only by his absence, who left an unfathomable void in my life. A pronounced taste for reading. A certain sexual precocity. And, most of all, an enormous need to be seen.

All the necessary elements were now in place.

Part Two

THE PREY

Consent: In moral philosophy: an act of free thought in which a person fully commits to accepting or accomplishing something.
In law: authorization for marriage given by the parents or guardian of a minor.

—Trésor de la langue française

ONE EVENING MY MOTHER DRAGGED ME ALONG TO A DINNER party to which some well-known literary figures had also been invited. Initially I refused to go point-blank. The company of her friends had become as excruciating to me as that of my classmates, from whom I was increasingly turning away. At the age of thirteen I was becoming a recluse. She insisted, grew angry, used emotional blackmail: I had to stop moping around on my own with my books, and anyway, what had her friends done to me, why didn't I want to see them anymore? Eventually I gave in.

He sat at the table at a forty-five-degree angle, a conspicuously striking presence. He was handsome, of indeterminate age; his head, scrupulously maintained, was entirely bald, which made him look a little like a Buddhist monk. His eyes followed my every movement, and when I finally dared to turn toward him, he threw me a smile, which I confused for a paternal smile, because it was the smile of a man, and I no longer had a father. With his brilliant comebacks and effortlessly well-chosen quotations, this man, who I soon realized was a writer, knew how to charm his audience, and clearly had an instinctive mastery of the strictly codified rules of Parisian social interaction. Every time he opened his mouth, his fellow guests hooted with laughter, but it was on me that his eyes—amused, mesmerizing—lingered. No man had ever looked at me like that before.

I caught his Slavic-sounding name in passing, which immediately aroused my curiosity. It was just a simple coincidence, but I owe my own surname, and a quarter of my blood, to the Bohemia of Kafka, whose *Metamorphosis* I had just read, enthralled; moreover, at this precise point in my adolescence, I considered Dostoyevsky's novels to be the absolute apex of literary achievement. A Russian surname, the lean physique of a Buddhist monk, preternaturally blue eyes—that was all it took to seize my attention.

Normally, during dinners like this, I would disappear off to another room, where I would let myself be lulled by the murmur of conversation, half listening, apparently distracted, but in reality acutely attentive. This particular evening, I had brought a book to read, and after the main course I took refuge in the small sitting room off the dining room where cheese was now being served (the interminable succession of courses, at no less interminable intervals). I was trying to read my book, but the words grew blurred, it was impossible to concentrate, and I suddenly sensed, from where he was sitting all the way at the other end of the room, G.'s eyes caressing my cheek. His voice, with its slight lilt, neither masculine nor feminine, insinuated itself inside me like a spell, an enchantment. Every inflection, every word, seemed addressed to me alone. Was I the only person to notice?

His presence was electric.

It was time to go. The moment—that I was afraid I'd only dreamed, the confusing feeling of being desired for the first time—was almost over. In a few minutes we'd say goodbye and I would never hear his name again. And then, as I was putting on my coat, I saw my mother flirting with the charming G., who was openly flirting back. I couldn't believe my eyes. Of course! How could I ever have imagined that this man could be interested in me, a teenage girl who was as unattractive as a toad?

G. and my mother exchanged a few more words. She laughed, flattered by his attentions, and then turned to me.

"Are you coming, darling? We're going to drop Michel first and then G. He lives quite near us. Then we'll be home."

G. sat next to me in the back seat of the car. Something

magnetic passed between us. He had his arm against mine, his eyes on me, and the predatory smile of a large golden wildcat. All conversation was redundant.

The book I had taken along with me that evening, the one I'd been reading in the small sitting room, was Balzac's *Eugénie Grandet*, which was to become, thanks to a play on words of which I was for a long time completely oblivious, the title of the human comedy in which I was to play the principal role: *l'ingénue grandit*—"the innocent grows up."

THE WEEK FOLLOWING OUR FIRST MEETING, I WAS DESPERATE to get to a bookshop. When I did, it was to buy one of G.'s books, though I was surprised when the bookseller advised against the one I'd selected at random and pointed me to a different work by the same author. "This one would be more suitable for you, I think," he said, rather enigmatically. A black-and-white photograph of G. punctuated a long frieze of portraits of writers in the same format, a shrine to all the important authors of the day, which ran around the four walls of the bookshop. I opened the book at the first page, and my eyes fell upon another unsettling coincidence: the first sentence—not the second, not the third, but the very first, the one the text opens with, the famous beginning with which generations of writers have struggled—began with my exact date of birth, the very day, month, and year: "On Thursday, 16 March 1972, the clock in the Luxembourg station chimed half past twelve." If that wasn't a sign! As excited as I was surprised, I left the bookshop clutching the precious volume under my arm, pressing it against my heart as though destiny had gifted it to me.

I devoured the novel over the next two days. Though it contained nothing shocking (the bookseller had chosen well), it did contain open allusions to the fact that the narrator was rather more susceptible to the beauty of young girls than that of women his own age. I stared into space, thinking how privileged I was to have met such a talented man of letters, so glamorous too (in truth, it was the memory of the way he looked at me that made my heart soar), and I began to see myself differently. Looking in the mirror now, I thought I was quite pretty. The toad, whose reflection used to make me flee what I saw in shop windows, vanished. How could I not feel flattered that a man—not any man, an actual "man of letters"—had deigned to lay his eyes on me? Since childhood, books had been my siblings, my companions, my tutors, my friends. With my blind veneration of the "Writer" with a capital "W," it was almost inevitable that I would conflate the man with his status as an artist.

I used to pick up the mail every day and take it up to the apartment. The gardienne would hand it to me when I walked in from school. One day, among a handful of official-looking envelopes, I saw my name and address inscribed in turquoise ink, with beautiful handwriting that sloped upward and slightly to the left, as if the words were trying to take flight. On the back, in the same cerulean ink, I read G.'s first and last names.

It was the first of what would be a great many letters, exquisitely charming and dripping with compliments. There was one important detail—G. always used the formal *vous*, just as if I were a grown-up. This was the first time that someone in my circle, apart from my schoolteachers, had ever used *vous* to address me, and it flattered my ego while at the same time instantly placing me on an equal footing with him. I didn't dare reply. But G. was not a man to be so easily discouraged. He sometimes wrote to me twice a day. I took to dropping into the gardienne's lodge morning and evening, terrified that my mother would come across one of these letters, which I kept on me at all times like a secret treasure, careful never to mention them to anyone. Eventually, after repeated solicitations, I plucked up the courage to pen a response to him, prim and shy but a response all the same. I had just turned fourteen. He was almost fifty. What of it?

No sooner had I nibbled at the bait than G. pounced. He began looking out for me in the street, wandering back and forth all over the neighborhood, trying to bring about an impromptu encounter, which occurred soon enough. We exchanged a few words, and then I walked home, dazed with love. I grew used to the possibility of bumping into him at any moment, so much so that his invisible presence accompanied me on my walk to school, on my way home, when I went shopping at the market or hung out with my friends. One day he sent me a letter arranging to meet. The telephone was far too dangerous, he wrote, it might be my mother who answered.

He asked me to meet him at Saint-Michel, by the number 27 bus stop. I was on time, and on edge, sensing that I was committing an enormous transgression. I'd imagined us going to a café somewhere in the neighborhood. To chat, get to know each other a bit. But as soon as he arrived, he told me he wanted to invite me to "afternoon tea" at his apartment. He'd bought some delicious pastries from a prohibitively expensive patisserie, whose name he uttered with greedy relish. All for me. Nonchalantly, he carried on talking as he crossed the street. I followed him mechanically, light-headed with words, and found myself at the stop for the same line going in the other direction. The bus pulled up. G. motioned me to get on, saying with a smile that I mustn't be afraid. His tone of voice was reassuring. "Nothing bad is going to happen to you!" My hesitation seemed to disappoint him.

I wasn't prepared for this. Incapable of reacting, caught off guard, I simply could not bear to seem like an idiot. Nor could I bear to be taken for a little kid who knew nothing about life. "You mustn't pay any attention to all the dreadful things people say about me. Come on, get on!" My hesitation had nothing to do with anything that anybody I knew had said. No one had said anything dreadful about him because I hadn't told anyone about our meeting.

As the bus sped down the Boulevard Saint-Michel and past the Luxembourg Gardens, G. smiled at me beatifically, threw me amorous, knowing glances, gazed at me adoringly. It was a beautiful day. Two stops later we pulled up to his apartment building. This wasn't what I had imagined either. Couldn't we walk for a while?

The staircase was narrow, there was no elevator, and we had to climb up to the sixth floor. "I live in a maid's room in the attic. I expect you imagine all writers to be very rich men; well, as you shall see, literature rarely provides enough to sustain a person. But I am very happy here. I live like a student and that suits me perfectly. Luxury and comfort do not breed inspiration."

There wasn't room to walk up six flights side by side. On the outside I was dreadfully calm, but inside my chest my heart was thumping like a drum.

He must have guessed I was afraid because he went ahead of me, presumably so I didn't feel trapped and still felt I could turn around and go back down. For a moment I imagined running away, but as we walked up the stairs, G. carried on chatting cheerfully, like a young man excited to be inviting a young girl up to his studio for the first time, having only just met her ten minutes earlier. His gait was agile, athletic; at no point did he appear out of breath. The physical condition of a sportsman.

The door opened onto an untidy studio with a spartan kitchen area at one end, so poky there was barely room for a chair. It had the means to make a cup of tea, but not so much as a pan to boil an egg.

"This is where I write," he declared solemnly. And there, on a tiny table wedged between the sink and the refrigerator, a pile of blank pages and a typewriter had pride of place. The room smelled of incense and dust. A ray of sunlight came through the window. A miniature bronze Buddha sat on a pedestal table that was missing a foot, propped up on a pile of books. A sad-looking elephant, its trunk aloft, a souvenir from a trip to India, seemed a little lost on the floor where a small Persian carpet skirted the parquet. A pair of Tunisian babouches, and books, more books, dozens of piles of books of all sizes, colors, thicknesses, and breadths, were strewn across the floor. G. invited me to sit down. There was only one place where two people could sit side by side—the bed.

Perched there, primly, my feet riveted to the floor, palms flat on my squeezed-together knees, back upright, I searched his face for a sign that would enlighten me as to the reason I was there. For several minutes my heart had been racing faster and faster, unless of course it was time itself whose rhythm had changed. I could have stood up and left. I wasn't afraid of G. He would never force me to stay against my will, I was sure of that. I felt an ineluctable shift in the situation and yet I didn't stand up, and I didn't say anything. G. was moving as if in a dream. I didn't see him come toward me, but suddenly he was there, sitting next to me, his arms around my trembling shoulders.

That first afternoon in his studio, G. behaved with exquisite delicacy. He kissed me tenderly, stroked my shoulders, slipped his hand under my sweater without asking me to take it off, though eventually I did. We were like two shy adolescents messing around in the back of a car. I lay there, languid but inhibited, incapable of the slightest movement, the faintest boldness. I concentrated on his lips, his mouth, touched his face with the tips of my fingers as he propped himself over me. Time stretched out until eventually, cheeks ablaze, lips and heart swollen with an utterly unfamiliar joy, I left and went home.

"I DON'T BELIEVE A WORD OF IT!"

"I promise you, it's true. Look, he's written me a poem."

My mother took the piece of paper I held out to her with a grimace of disgust mingled with incredulity. She looked horrified but also a tiny bit jealous. After all, when she'd offered to give the writer a lift home that evening, and when he'd accepted in such suave tones, she could well have imagined that he wasn't entirely impervious to her charms. At first, stunned by the revelation that I had, somewhat precociously, become her rival, she refused to believe it. She swiftly regained her composure, and then spat out a word I could not believe could be associated with G.:

"Are you aware he's a pedophile?"

"A *what*? Is that why you offered to give him a lift home, and let him sit in the back with your daughter?"

Without missing a beat, she told me she was going to send me to boarding school. Beneath the rafters, our screams flew thick and fast. How could she think of depriving me of this, my first, my last, my only love? Did she really imagine that, having deprived me of my father (because, obviously, now it was all her fault), I was going to allow her to do it a second time? I would never agree to be apart from him. I would rather die.

THE LETTERS KEPT COMING, EACH MORE PASSIONATE THAN the last. G. declared his love for me in every possible way, begged me to come back and see him as soon as I could, vowed he couldn't live without me, that life wasn't worth living a moment longer if he wasn't in my arms. Overnight I had turned into a goddess.

The following Saturday I told my mother I was going to a friend's house to study. I rang at G.'s door. How could I resist that wolfish smile, those laughing eyes, the long, slender, aristocratic fingers?

A few minutes later I was lying on his bed, and this was something quite unlike anything I had ever known. This wasn't Julien's skinny, hairless body next to mine, his velvety, adolescent skin, the acrid odor of his sweat. This was a man's body. Strong, stubbly, freshly washed and smelling of eau de cologne.

Our first encounter had been devoted to the upper part of my body. This time he ventured, intrepid, toward more intimate regions. And for that he had to undo my shoelaces, a task he undertook with undisguised pleasure, before pulling off my jeans and my cotton panties (I didn't own any feminine underwear worthy of the name, and it appeared that nothing could have delighted G. more, though at the time I was only dimly aware of this).

In a mellifluous voice he boasted of his experience, how skillfully he had taken the virginity of several young teenage girls, how he always ensured it didn't hurt in the slightest; he even claimed they would recall it with emotion as long as they lived, aware of how lucky they were to have met him and not another person, someone rough and careless who would have pinned them unceremoniously to the mattress so that they would forever have associated that unique moment with a feeling of regret.

Except that, as it turned out, he was unable to penetrate me. With an instinctive reflex, my thighs jammed tight together. I howled with pain before he even touched me—despite the fact this was the one thing I'd been dreaming of. In a confusion of bravado and romance, I had already secretly determined the inevitable outcome—G. would be my first lover. That was the reason I was lying on his bed. So why was my body refusing? Why this intractable fright?

G. was undaunted. He murmured reassuringly:

"Don't worry. We can do it another way, you know."

Just as one must cross oneself with holy water before entering a church, taking possession of the body and soul of a young girl cannot be done without a certain sense of the sacred, a timeless ritual. Sodomy has its rules, and must be carefully, religiously, prepared.

G. flipped me over on the mattress and set about licking

every single part of my body from top to toe: back of my neck, shoulders, back, hips, buttocks. Something of my presence in the world dissolved. And, while his greedy tongue insinuated itself inside me, my soul took flight.

That is how I lost the first part of my virginity. *Just like a little boy*, he whispered to me in a soft voice.

I WAS IN LOVE. I FELT ADORED AS NEVER BEFORE. AND that was enough to efface all my sullenness, and to suspend any judgment about our relationship.

After we'd been to bed, in those early days, there were two things I found particularly touching: seeing G. stand up to pee and watching him shave. It was as if those activities were, for the first time, part of my world, for too long restricted to feminine rituals.

What I discovered in G.'s embrace, the hitherto unfathomable domain of adult sexuality, was a whole new continent to me. I explored this male body with the concentration of a privileged disciple. I absorbed his lessons with gratitude, and I worked hard on my practical exercises. I felt I had been chosen.

G. confessed to me that he had until recently led a rather dissolute life, as some of his books bore out. He kneeled before me, his eyes misted with tears, and promised to break up with all his other mistresses, whispering that he had never in his whole life been so happy, that meeting me was a *miracle*, a veritable gift from the gods.

At the beginning, G. took me to museums and the theater,

gave me records, told me what books to read. We would spend hours walking hand in hand along the paths in the Luxembourg Gardens, wandering the streets of Paris, ignoring all the looks—curious, suspicious, disapproving, sometimes openly hostile—of the people walking by us.

I don't recall my parents often coming to pick me up from school, even when I was still at an age when I would wait, with a delicious squirm of anxiety, for the doors to open to one or the other of their beloved faces. My mother always worked late. I went home on my own after class. My father didn't even know the name of the street where my school was.

Now G. waited outside school for me almost every day. Not right in front, but a few meters away, on the little square at the end of the street, so that I could spot him straightaway just beyond the crowd of overexcited teenagers. In springtime, his rangy silhouette was wrapped in a colonial-style safari jacket; in winter, an overcoat like those of Russian officers in the Second World War, full-length and covered in gold buttons. He wore sunglasses, summer and winter, to protect his anonymity.

Ours was a forbidden love. Reviled by all decent people. I knew this, because he told me so repeatedly. It meant I wasn't allowed to tell anyone. I had to be careful. But why? Why, if I loved him and he loved me?

And were those sunglasses really so discreet?

AFTER EACH SESSION OF LOVEMAKING, DURING WHICH G. feasted on my body like a starving man, the two of us would lie in the calm of his studio, surrounded by so many hundreds of books it made me dizzy. He would hold me in his arms like a newborn baby, run his hands through my disheveled hair, call me his "beloved child," his "beautiful schoolgirl," and softly recount the long history of illicit love affairs between young girls and middle-aged men.

I now had a private tutor entirely dedicated to my education. The extent of his cultural knowledge was mesmerizing, and my admiration was, if possible, increasing, even if the reality was that the lessons I received after school were always very specifically oriented.

"Are you aware that in ancient times, the sexual initiation of young people by adults was not only encouraged, it was considered a duty? Even as late as the nineteenth century—little Virginia was only thirteen when she married Edgar Allan Poe, did you know that? And when I think about all those respectable parents reading *Alice in Wonderland* to their children before bed, without having the faintest idea of who Lewis Carroll was, it makes me want to howl with laughter. He was obsessed with photography, it was quite compulsive, he took hundreds of photographs of little girls, including the real Alice, the love of his life, who inspired his masterpiece. Have you ever seen them?"

In a large book of photography prominently displayed on his shelves, he showed me the erotic pictures that Irina Ionesco had taken of her daughter Eva when she was just eight years old, her legs spread, dressed only in black stockings that ended mid-thigh, her gorgeous doll-like face made up like a prostitute. (He omitted to tell me that her mother subsequently lost custody of Eva and that, aged thirteen, she was placed with social services.)

Another time, he ranted about Americans, mired in sexual frustration, persecuting poor Roman Polanski and trying to stop him from making films.

"They're such puritans, they insist on conflating everything. That girl who claims she was raped was manipulated by people who were jealous of his success. It's obvious she consented. And what about David Hamilton—do you think all his models would have offered themselves up to the lens of his camera if they hadn't had one thing on their minds? You'd have to be absurdly naïve to believe such a thing."

The litany of examples was endless. Faced with so many similarly edifying examples, how could I disagree? A fourteen-year-old girl has the right and the liberty to love whom she wants. I understood the lesson very well. And even better, I had become a muse.

TO START WITH, MY MOTHER WAS NOT THRILLED BY THE situation. But once she got over her surprise and shock, she consulted her friends and took advice from people around her; no one, apparently, was particularly disturbed. Eventually, in the face of my resolve, she came around. Perhaps she thought I was stronger and more mature than I was. Perhaps she was too alone to act differently. Perhaps she needed a man by her side, someone to father her daughter, to stand up to this anomaly, this aberration, this . . . thing. Someone to take charge.

It would also have helped if the cultural context and the times had been less liberal.

Ten years before I met G., toward the end of the 1970s, a large number of left-wing newspapers and intellectuals regularly came to the defense of adults accused of having had "shameful" relationships with adolescents. In 1977, an open letter in support of the decriminalization of sexual relations between minors and adults, entitled "Regarding a Trial," was published in the newspaper *Le Monde*, signed by a number of eminent intellectuals, psychoanalysts, well-known philosophers, and writers at the peak of their careers, largely from the left. They included Roland Barthes, Gilles Deleuze, Simone de Beauvoir, Jean-Paul Sartre, André Glucksmann, and Louis Aragon. The letter argued against the detention of three men awaiting trial for having had (and photographed) sexual relations with two minors aged thirteen and fourteen: "Such a lengthy preventative detention to investigate a straightforward affair of 'morality,' in which the children were not in any way victims of violence—indeed, on the contrary, they assured the judges that they were consenting (even if the current law denies them the capacity to consent)—seems to us genuinely scandalous."

The petition was also signed by G.M. But it was not until 2013 that he revealed that he had in fact both initiated and drafted it, and, furthermore, that he had encountered very few negative responses in his quest for signatories (notable among those who refused to sign were Marguerite Duras, Hélène Cixous, and . . . Michel Foucault, who was not exactly the last person to denounce all such forms of repression). The same year, another petition was published in *Le Monde*, entitled "A Call for the Revision of the Penal Code Regarding Relationships Between Minors and Adults," which garnered even more support (to name but a few, Françoise Dolto, Louis Althusser, and Jacques Derrida added their support, along with most of those who had signed the earlier petition; the open letter was signed by eighty people, including some of the most high-profile public intellectuals of the era). Yet another petition appeared in 1979 in *Libération*, in support of one Gérard R., accused of living with girls aged between six and twelve, also signed by several well-known literary figures.

Thirty years on, all the newspapers that had printed these exceedingly dubious opinion pieces went on to publish, one after the other, their mea culpa, arguing that in any period of history, the media merely reflects the ideas of the time.

So why did all these left-wing intellectuals so passionately defend positions that today seem so shocking to us? Particularly the relaxing of the penal code concerning sexual relations between adults and minors, and the abolition of the age of consent?

The reason is that in the 1970s, in the name of free love and the sexual revolution, everyone was supposed to be in favor of the liberation of physical pleasure. Repressing juvenile sexuality was considered to be a form of social oppression, and limiting sexual relationships to those between individuals of the same age range constituted a form of segregation. The fight against any curb on desire, any kind of repression, was the watchword of the era; no one spoke up against it, except for a few strait-laced puritans and reactionary tribunals.

A generation adrift, suffering from a blindness for which nearly all the signatories of these petitions would later apologize.

During the 1980s, the intellectual circle in which I was growing up was still marked by this vision of the world. When she was an adolescent, my mother told me, the body and its desires were still taboo, and her parents never talked to her about sex at all. Having just turned eighteen in May 1968, she first had to free herself from her corseted upbringing, and then from the hold of an unbearable husband whom she married far too young. Like the heroines of Jean-Luc Godard and Claude Sautet's movies, she now aspired above all to live life according to her own rules. "It's forbidden to forbid" remained, it seemed, her mantra. It's not easy to escape the zeitgeist.

This, then, was the context in which my mother eventually came around to the presence of G. in our lives. It was utter madness for her to give us her absolution. I think, deep down, she knew that. Did she also realize that she risked one day being severely criticized, first and foremost by her own daughter? Was I so fiercely obstinate that she was unable to stand up to me? Whatever the reason, her only intervention was to make a pact with G. He had to swear that he would never make me suffer. It was he who told me this. I can just imagine the scene, the two of them looking each other straight in the eye with great solemnity. "Say it: 'I swear!'"

She sometimes invited him for dinner in our little attic apartment. The three of us would sit around the table, eating lamb and green beans, as though we were playing happy families, daddy-mommy, reunited at the end of the day, with me sitting radiantly between them, the holy trinity, together again.

As shocking and abnormal as it might seem, perhaps G. was

for her, subconsciously, the ideal paternal substitute, the father she had been unable to give me.

And on top of it all, this kind of scandalous situation was not entirely displeasing to her. There was even something gratifying about it. In our bohemian world of artists and intellectuals, deviations from conventional morality were viewed with a certain level of tolerance, even admiration. And G. was a well-known writer, which made it altogether rather flattering.

In a different social circle, one in which artists didn't exercise the same fascination, things would no doubt have turned out differently. The monsieur would have been threatened with being sent to prison. The girl would have been sent to a psychologist, might perhaps have brought up a buried memory of the snap of elastic on a tanned thigh in a Moroccan restaurant, and the whole thing would have been dealt with. End of story.

"Your grandparents must never find out, my darling. They wouldn't understand," my mother said to me one day, quite lightly, in the middle of a conversation.

for her subconsciously the ideal paternal substituted the father she had been unable to give me.

And on top of it all, this kind of scandalous situation was not entirely displeasing to her. There was even something gratifying about it. In our bohemian world of artists and intellectuals, deviance from conventional morality were viewed with a certain level of tolerance, even admiration. And G. was a well-known writer, which made it altogether rather flattering.

In a different social circle, one in which artists didn't exercise the same fascination, things would no doubt have turned out differently. The monsieur would have been threatened with being sent to prison. The girl would have been sent to a psychologist, might perhaps have brought up a buried memory of the strap of elastic on a tanned thigh in a Moroccan restaurant, and the whole thing would have been dealt with. End of story.

Your grandparents must never find out, my darling. They wouldn't understand, my mother said to me one day, quite lightly, in the middle of a conversation.

THE GNAWING PAIN BEGAN ONE EVENING, IN THE JOINT of the thumb of my left hand. I suppose I must have knocked my hand without noticing; I tried to work out what intense manual activity I had done that day, but nothing came to mind. Two hours later the swelling evolved into an almost unendurable burning sensation, radiating through the joints of all my fingers. How was it possible that such a tiny part of my body could hurt so badly? Worried, my mother called the emergency doctor, who sent me for a blood test. The results showed an abnormally raised level of white blood cells. We were sent to the emergency room. By the time we got there, the pain had spread to the joints of all my limbs. Even before they found me a bed, I could no longer move. I was literally paralyzed. A doctor diagnosed acute rheumatic fever, triggered by a streptococcal infection.

I had to remain in the hospital for several weeks, which I remember as interminable, but illness has a tendency to distort the perception of time.

During my stay in the hospital, three unexpected visits left me with recollections that are respectively amusing, embarrassing, and devastating. The first took place only a few days after I was hospitalized. My mother (or might it have been one of her friends, motivated by the best of intentions?) wasted no time in introducing the patient to a psychoanalyst who, it was clear from the very first look he gave me when he walked into the room, was a deeply compassionate man. I had already met him two or three times at various dinner parties I'd been to with my mother.

"V., I've just come to chat to you, I think it might do you some good."

"What do you mean?"

"I think your illness is the manifestation of something else. A more deep-seated ailment, if you understand what I mean. How are things at school? Are you doing well?"

"No, it's a nightmare. I almost never go. I skip all the classes I don't like, which drives my mother crazy. I forge her signature on notes to the teachers, then sit and smoke in a café for the rest of the day. One time I even pretended it was my grandfather's funeral, and she got really mad! I can't deny I went a bit far there."

"I wonder if this illness might have something to do with your . . . current situation."

There. He'd said it. No more beating around the bush. What did he think, that it was G. who'd given me strep throat?

"What situation? What are you talking about?"

"Shall we start with how you were feeling before you fell ill? Do you want to try to talk about it? I think you're smart enough to understand that talking is a way of beginning to get better. What do you think?"

Of course, as soon as I began to sense a genuine interest in my lowly self—and what's more, from a member of the male sex—all my defenses crumbled.

"All right."

"So why are you not going to classes? Do you think it's just because you're bored in certain subjects? I wonder if there's another reason."

"I'm, well, I'm kind of . . . scared of people. Isn't that pathetic?"

"Not at all. Lots of people are like you, they have panic attacks in certain situations. School, especially at your age, can be very anxiety-provoking, especially in such circumstances. What about the pain, where is it now?"

"My knees . . . it's horrible, it's like they're burning on the inside."

"That's what your mother said. It's very interesting."

"Really? My knees are interesting?"

"Have you noticed something about the word 'knee'? The way it rhymes with 'me' and 'we'? You're suffering from joint pain, are you not? So, would you agree if I said that you're also suffering pain in the joint between the 'me' and the 'we'?"

With these words, the psychoanalyst's face lit up with an expression of intense satisfaction. He looked almost in a state of bliss. My knees had never provoked such an effect on G. I didn't know what to say.

"Sometimes psychic pain, when it remains silent, expresses itself through the body by triggering physical pain. Why don't you have a think about all this? I don't want to tire you out, especially when it is so important that you rest. Let's leave it for today."

Apart from, perhaps, a vague allusion at the beginning of

our conversation, the psychoanalyst hadn't said a word about my relationship with G. Thinking he was just another sanctimonious moralizer, as G. liked to dismiss anyone who cast disapproving glances in our direction, I said, provocatively,

"So you have nothing more to say about my 'situation'?"

In a clipped tone of voice, he replied:

"I could say more, but you wouldn't like it. Rheumatism isn't really something girls of your age tend to suffer from, you know."

A few days later, it was the turn of my mother's lover to turn up unexpectedly at my bedside. With his moustache and elegant collection of bow ties, he had never shown me any particular sign of affection. And now, here he was, on his own, with a serious, grave expression on his face. What could he want of me? Had no one told me I was at death's door? Was that why I was arousing such pity? Without waiting for permission, he sat down in a chair on the right-hand side of the bed and, with an affectionate gesture that I didn't recognize, he took my hand in his, which was large, warm, and slightly clammy.

"How are you feeling, my darling V.?"

"Okay, fine . . . you know, it depends on the day."

"Your mother tells me you were in terrible pain. You're so brave, you know. It's so good you're being looked after here. The children's hospital is the best there is."

"It's nice of you to have come." (Though actually I hadn't the faintest idea what he was doing there.)

"Don't be silly. Of course I came. I know I've rather monopolized your mother the last few years, and I don't suppose you see me as a friend. But . . . how can I put it . . . I'd like . . . you know, given your father's complete absence, I feel a bit guilty not to have been more involved in your life. I'd like to have more of a role, but I'm not sure how to go about it."

I smiled, a little taken aback. But deep down I was touched. At last he let go of my hand and, with a desperate glance around the white walls of my room, seemed to be searching for inspiration to continue his monologue. Eventually he found unexpected support in a book that was sitting on my bedside table.

"Do you like Proust? How wonderful. He's my favorite writer, did you know that?"

G. had given me the first volume of *Remembrance of Things Past*. "There's nothing like illness to understand the work of poor Marcel," he explained. "He wrote lying down on his sickbed, between coughing fits."

"I've just started . . . I'm enjoying it. I'm not so keen on all those duchesses, mind you, but all the romantic passion is really moving."

"Absolutely! Romantic passion! That's it! Actually, I wanted to tell you. Things with your mother aren't like they were. I think we're going to split up."

"Oh, right, so that means you were together? News to me."

"Right, well, yes, um, you know what I mean. But I'd like to stay in touch with you. We could have lunch together."

Then he looked at his pocket watch (of course!) and announced that, unfortunately, he had to go. He stood up and leaned over to give me a goodbye kiss. In a sudden involuntary movement, his head tipped and his great big purple mouth with its coarse moustache landed slap bang on my lips. Scarlet with embarrassment, he pulled away, not knowing where to put himself, and disappeared as if pursued by a ghost.

Subconscious acts implicate only those who pick up on them, as my new psychoanalyst friend might have put it.

How to know if it was intentional or not? My mother's lover's suggestion had appeared sincere, but this sideslip of a kiss cast doubt on his motives.

Two days later, I was blindsided by yet another impromptu visit. Clearly there was no way I was going to be left in peace while in the hospital; the place was an open house. A face that I'd been trying to forget for the last three years suddenly appeared in the doorway. It was my father, with that stubbornly ironic expression of his that drove me mad. The pain in my joints had kept me from sleeping for much of the night. I was exhausted and tense. What was he thinking: that he would just turn up and, as if by magic, I'd forget everything? All those years of silence, the hours I'd spent crying as I tried to get hold of him by phone, his new wife or his secretary assuring me he couldn't be reached, he was awfully busy, away on business, and who knows what else.

No, there'd been a clean break, and I had nothing else to say to him.

"What are you doing here? Have you suddenly remembered you have a daughter?"

"Your mother called me because she's worried about you. She told me you're suffering terribly, and no one knows how you caught this strep infection. I thought you'd be happy to see me."

If I'd been able to move, I'd have pushed him out the door by force.

"What difference does it make to you that I'm ill?"

"I thought you'd be pleased, that's all. I am your father, you know."

"I don't need you anymore, okay?" The words burst out in spite of myself.

And then suddenly it all came out in a rush:

"I've met someone."

"You've met someone? What do you mean? You're in love?"

"Yes! And that means you can go now, and carry on living your little life in peace without me, because finally I've found someone who cares about me."

"I see. Don't you think you're a little young, at fourteen, to be having that kind of relationship? Who is he, anyway?"

"Well, you're not going to believe it, because he's a writer, he's wonderful, and the most amazing thing is, he loves me. He's called G.M. Does that mean anything to you?"

"What? That sleazy piece of shit? You've got to be fucking kidding me."

I'd got him. I flashed him a smug smile. But his reaction was dramatic. Overwhelmed by uncontrollable rage, he grabbed a metal chair, lifted it over his head, and threw it against the wall. With the back of his hand he swept some medical instruments lying on a table to the floor, and then began yelling, reeling off a volley of insults, calling me a little whore, a slut, ranting that he wasn't remotely surprised at what I'd become, with a mother like mine, she couldn't be trusted, she was nothing but a whore as well. He spat out his disgust for G., that monster, that piece of shit, he swore he would turn him in to the police the minute he left the hospital. Alerted by all the noise, a nurse entered the room and, frowning, asked him to either calm down or leave the premises immediately.

My father grabbed his cashmere coat and left. The walls were still shaking from his yelling. I lay there, prostrate, ostensibly in shock, but in reality not at all dissatisfied by the effect I'd had on him.

If this declaration was not what psychoanalysts call a cry for help, then I don't know what it was. No need to point out that my father never did file a complaint against G. and that I never heard from him again. It turned out, in fact, quite the opposite: my revelation furnished him with the perfect alibi for his innate negligence.

The weeks dragged on in the gloomy hospital, where G. came to see me almost every day and no one batted an eyelid. Happily, the doctors eventually found a remedy for my swollen joints. And before I left one more episode took place that deserves to be told.

I was encouraged to make the most of my stay in this highly respected pediatric medical establishment, with a consultation with the resident gynecologist. The doctor, a very solicitous man, quizzed me about my sexual activity and, in a surprising display of trust (always this girlishness when faced with the charm of a pleasant deep voice, and a sincere display of interest), I ended up confessing that I was on the pill, having met a lovely boy, but that I was suffering from a complete inability to give myself to him, terrified of the pain of being deflowered. (For several weeks, all of G.'s attempts to get over my difficulties had been in vain. Which did not appear to bother him a great deal, my buttocks appearing to satisfy him amply.) The doctor raised an eyebrow, a little surprised, then declared that I appeared to be somewhat advanced for a girl my age, and that he was willing to help me. He examined me and declared, categorically and happily, that I was indeed the "Virgin incarnate," for he had never seen a hymen so intact. Conscientiously, he immediately suggested a small incision under local anesthetic, which would finally allow me to discover the joy of sex.

Apparently, information did not circulate between the different departments of the hospital, and I choose to believe that the doctor had no idea what he was about to do: help the man who visited my bedside every day to ejaculate freely in every orifice of my body.

I don't know if it qualifies as medical rape or an act of torture. But whatever it was, at a—deft and painless—stroke, I finally became a woman.

Part Three

THE STRANGLEHOLD

"What captivates me is not so much a specific sex, but rather extreme youth, the age between ten and sixteen, which seems to me to be—more than what we usually mean by this phrase—to be the real "third sex."

—G.M., "Under Sixteen"

THERE ARE NUMEROUS WAYS TO STEAL A PERSON'S SELF-hood. Some appear quite innocent at the outset.

One day, G. decided he wanted to help me with an essay. My grades were usually very good, especially in French, and I never felt the need to discuss my schoolwork with him. But that afternoon, obstinate as a mule, and in a particularly cheerful mood, he had already and without asking opened my homework notebook at my task for the following day.

"Have you done your essay yet? You know I can help you. You've left it a bit late if you're to hand it in tomorrow. So . . . let's see: 'Describe one of your achievements.'"

"No, don't worry, I've already thought about it, I'm going to do it in a bit."

"But why? Don't you want me to help you? It will take less time, and the sooner you're done, the sooner . . ."

He slid his hand under my shirt and gently stroked my left breast.

"Stop it! You're obsessed!"

"Well, let me tell you, by the time I was your age I'd done something truly extraordinary. Did you know I was a three-day event champion? I was! And one day . . ."

"I don't care. It's my essay."

G. scowled, then ensconced himself against the pillows at the end of the bed.

"Very well, as you wish. I shall read a bit, since my adolescence doesn't interest you."

Contrite, I leaned over him to give him a kiss, in the guise of an apology.

"Of course your life interests me, everything about you interests me, you know that."

G. sat up again.

"Is that true? So, you do want to hear! And we'll write it at the same time!"

"You're impossible! You're like a kid! Anyway, my teacher will know immediately that I didn't write it."

"No, we'll make it about a girl, and we'll use the kind of words you use, she won't notice a thing."

So, hunched over a piece of A4 paper with large pale blue squares and a thin red line for the margin, I began to take down G.'s dictation, in my delicate, neat handwriting, studious as always, the story of a young girl who managed to jump ten extremely challenging obstacles in a few minutes without knocking down or even brushing a single bar, sitting straight up on her mount, cheered on by a crowd of spectators transfixed by her proficiency, elegance, and precision of movement. I learned an entire vocabulary hitherto unknown to me, words whose meanings I had to keep asking him, for I'd only been on a horse once in my short life, and afterward I'd been rushed off to the doctor covered in eczema, coughing and weeping from the edema that had made my scarlet face swell to twice its size.

The next day, I shamefacedly handed my essay to my French teacher. The following week she returned it, exclaiming (whether or not she suspected anything I shall never know):

"You've surpassed yourself this week, V.! Nineteen out of twenty, there's nothing to add, it's the best grade in the class. Listen to me, the rest of you, I'm going to pass your classmate's homework around and I would like you all to read it carefully. And let it be a lesson to the lot of you. I hope it won't bother you, V., especially as your friends will find out what a brilliant horsewoman you are!"

And so the dispossession began.

After this, G. showed no more interest in my schoolwork, never encouraged me to write, or pushed me to think about what I might like to do with my life.

He was the writer.

down G.'s dictation in my delicate, neat handwriting, writing out, as always, the story of a young girl who managed to jump seven extremely challenging obstacles in a few minutes without knocking down or even touching a single bar, sitting straight upon her mount, cheered on by a crowd of spectators stunned by her proficiency, elegance, and precision of movement. I learned an entire vocabulary hitherto unknown to me, words whose meanings I had to keep asking him, for I'd only been on a horse once in my short life, and afterward I'd been rushed to the doctor suffering from eczema, coughing and sneezing from the edema that had made my swollen face swell to twice its size.

The next day, I triumphantly handed my essay to my French teacher. The following week she returned it. As for knowing whether or not she suspected anything, I shall never know.

"You've surpassed yourself this week, V.! Nineteen out of twenty, there's nothing to add. It's the best grade in the class. Listen to this, the rest of you. I'm going to pass your classmate's homework around and I would like you all to read it carefully. And may it be a lesson to the lot of you. I hope it won't bother you, V., especially as your friends will find out what a brilliant horsewoman you are."

And so the dispossession began.

After that, G. showed no more interest in my schoolwork, never encouraged me to write, or pushed me to think about what I might like to do with my life.

He was there, then.

AMONG MY VERY SMALL CIRCLE OF FRIENDS, THE REACtions to G. were confusing. The boys felt a visceral disgust for him, which suited G., because he had no desire whatsoever to get to know them. He preferred hairless prepubescent boys, no older than twelve, as I was soon to find out. Any older and they were no longer objects of pleasure; they were rivals.

Conversely, all the girls dreamed of meeting him. One day a girl asked me if he would read a story she'd written. Nothing could be more valuable than a "professional" writer's opinion. The adolescent girls of my era were a lot more brazen than their parents imagined. A fact that obviously delighted G.

One day I turned up late to school as usual. The music lesson had already begun, and everyone was standing and singing in unison. A scrap of paper, folded in four, landed on my desk next to my pencil case. I unfolded it and read: "He's cheating on you." Two grinning heads, fingers raised above their skulls, mimed two twisting horns. At the end of the lesson, as the students rushed all together to the door, I tried to flee, but one of the jokers caught up with me and whispered in my ear: "I saw the old man you're going out with on the bus, kissing another girl." I started to shake and tried to hide it. The boy threw me with one last comment: "My dad told me he's a stinking pedophile." I'd heard the word before, of course, without ever wondering whether it was true or not. Now, for the first time, it stabbed me through the heart. First, because it referred to the man I loved, and labeled him a criminal. And then, from the boy's tone of voice, oozing with contempt, I realized he had spontaneously placed me not in the camp of the victims, but in that of the accessories to the crime.

G. PROTESTED WHEN I TOLD HIM THAT SOME OF THE people in my circle of friends called him a "sex maniac." The expression troubled me. I considered his love for me to be of a sincerity that was above suspicion. Over time, I had read a few of his books—just the ones he recommended I read. The uncontroversial ones: the dictionary of philosophy that had just come out, and a few of the novels, though not all; he warned me off the more notorious ones. With a strength of conviction worthy of the finest politician, he swore, hand on heart, that those works no longer corresponded to the man he had become, thanks to me. Above all, he said, he was afraid that some pages might shock me. He said all this with the air of an innocent lamb.

I obeyed the ban for a long time. A couple of these forbidden books sat on the bookshelf by the bed, and their titles taunted me whenever I caught sight of them. But, like Bluebeard's wife, I'd made a promise and I would stick to my word. Presumably because I didn't have a nun watching over me to keep me on the straight and narrow if ever the idea of transgressing the forbidden crossed my mind.

Whenever I heard the terrible accusations made against him, some boundless naïveté made me believe that G. had created a fictional caricature of himself; that his books were a twisted exaggeration of the person he really was, that he demeaned himself in them, made himself look ugly, as a kind of provocation, like a larger-than-life character in a novel. A modern-day version of Dorian Gray's portrait, his work was the receptacle of all his faults, a way of allowing him to return to his life revitalized, untouched, ironed out, pure.

How could he be a bad person, if I loved him? Thanks to him, I was no longer the little girl waiting on her own in a restaurant for her daddy to turn up. Thanks to him, at last, I existed.

That lack, that lack of love, like the thirst that makes a man drink down to the last drop, the thirst of a junkie who doesn't check the quality of what he's scored, who injects himself with a lethal dose with the conviction that it will make him feel better. Relief, recognition, rapture.

WE HAD BEEN CORRESPONDING BY LETTER SINCE THE beginning of our relationship, just like, I told myself naïvely, in the time of *Les Liaisons dangereuses*. G. had encouraged me to use this mode of communication from the start, partly because he was a writer, but also as a matter of security, and of course to protect our love from prying eyes and ears. I didn't object; I was more comfortable in written than spoken language. I found it a natural way to express myself. I was very reserved with my classmates; I couldn't bear to speak in public, to stand up in front of the class and give a presentation. I was incapable of participating in any theatrical or artistic activity that required that I expose my body to be looked at by other people. The internet and the mobile phone didn't exist yet. The telephone inspired only disdain in G., who considered it a vulgar object devoid of any poetry. I kept the stack of flamboyant love letters that he used to send me whenever he went away, or when we hadn't been able to see each other for a few days, carefully bound with ribbon in an old cardboard box. I know he treasured mine just as carefully. But when I began to read his books (still avoiding the most salacious), I realized that I was far from holding exclusive rights to these epistolary outpourings.

Two of his books recount G.'s tumultuous love affairs with a bevy of young girls whose advances he was apparently unable to refuse. These girlfriends of his were all very demanding, and, unable to work out how to extricate himself from them, he began juggling, in a truly acrobatic fashion, increasingly barefaced lies so that he could keep two, three, or even four trysts with his lovers in the same day.

Not only did G. not hesitate to reproduce in his books the letters he received from his conquests, but they all seemed strangely familiar: in their style, their enthusiasm, and even their vocabulary, it was as if they constituted a single body spread out across the years, in which the distant voice of a single idealized young girl, composed of all the others, could be heard. Each letter bore witness to a love as spiritual as that between Heloise and Abelard, and as carnal as that between Valmont and Tourvel. It was like reading the naïve, antiquated prose of lovers from a different century. These weren't words of contemporary young women, but the universal and timeless terms taken from the epistolary literature of love. G. whispered them to us by stealth, breathing them onto our very tongues. He dispossessed us of our own words.

My own letters to G. do not stand out at all. Don't all vaguely "literary" teenage girls between fourteen and eighteen write in exactly the same way? Or was I influenced by the uniform style of these love letters after I'd read some of the ones in G.'s books? I can't help wondering if I was instinctively conforming to what you might call a "technical specification."

With hindsight, I realize he was taking us all for fools: by reproducing from one book to the next letters from young girls in the full flower of youth, all with the same obsessiveness, G. was establishing not only an image of himself as seducer but also, more perniciously, testimony that he was not the monster people said he was. All these declarations of love were proof that he was loved, and, better still, that he knew how to love. What a hypocritical way it was of going about things, deceiving not only his young mistresses but also his readers. I eventually saw through the function of the dozens of letters he had written to me, frenetically, since our first meeting. For G., loving adolescents was also about being a writer, and the authority and the psychological hold he enjoyed were all that was needed for his nymphet of the moment to confirm in writing that she was fulfilled. A letter leaves a trace, and the recipient feels duty-bound to respond, and when it is composed with passionate lyricism, she must show herself to be worthy of it. With this silent injunction, the teenage girl would give herself the mission of reassuring G. regarding all the pleasure he gave her, so that in the event of a raid by the police, there could be no doubt that she was a consenting partner. He was, of course, a past master in the execution of the faintest caress. The unequaled heights of our orgasmic pleasure were proof of that!

Such declarations, from the young virgins who ended up in G.'s bed and hadn't the slightest point of comparison, were actually rather comical.

Which was too bad for those devoted readers of his published diaries who let themselves be taken in.

BOWING TO FINANCIAL NECESSITY, G. PUBLISHED, WITH the precision of a metronome, one book a year. For several weeks he had been writing about us, our love story, and about what he called his "redemption." It was to be a novel inspired by our meeting, which would, he said, be a magnificent account of a "stellar" love affair, of the way he had turned his dissipated lifestyle around for the beautiful eyes of a fourteen-year-old girl. What a romantic subject! Don Juan, cured of his sexual frenzy, determined no longer to be dominated by his urges, vowing that he was a changed man, upon whom mercy had alighted along with Cupid's arrow.

Happy, excited, and focused, he sat at his typewriter writing up notes from his black Moleskine notebook. The same one as Hemingway used, he told me. I was still strictly forbidden to read his diary, which was both private and literary. But since G. had begun writing his novel, reality had swapped sides: I was gradually turning from a muse into a fictional character.

BOWING TO FINANCIAL NECESSITY, G. PUBLISHED, WITH the precision of a metronome, one book a year. For several weeks he had been writing about us, our love story, and about what he called his "redemption." It was to be a novel inspired by our meeting, which would, he said, be a magnificent account of this "stellar" love affair, of the way he had turned his dissipated lifestyle around for the beautiful eyes of a fourteen-year-old girl. What a romantic subject: Don Juan cured of his sexual frenzy, determined no longer to be dominated by his urges, vowing that he was a changed man, upon whom mercy had alighted along with Cupid's arrow.

Happily settled, and focused, he sat at his typewriter writing up notes from his black Moleskine notebook. The same one as Hemingway used, he told me. I was still strictly forbidden to read his diary, which was both private and literary. But since G. had begun writing his novel, reality had swapped sides: I was gradually turning from a muse into a fictional character in

G. WAS SUBDUED AND UNSMILING, WHICH WAS NOT LIKE him at all. We'd met up in one of our favorite cafés, opposite the Luxembourg Gardens. When I asked him what was eating him, he hesitated for a moment before admitting the truth. That morning he'd received a summons from the Juvenile Squad, after an anonymous letter concerning him had been received by them. It appeared we were not the only people to be sensitive to the charms of epistolary communication.

G. had spent the afternoon stashing all my letters and photographs (and quite possibly other things that were similarly compromising) in a safe-deposit box at his lawyer's office. The summons was for the following week. Obviously, it concerned us, me. Legally, the age of consent was fifteen. I was a long way from turning fifteen. The situation was serious. We had to be prepared for every possible scenario. Had times changed? Were attitudes less liberal now?

The following Thursday my mother, her stomach in a knot of anxiety, sat waiting for news of the interview. She was aware that her responsibility as a parent was at stake. Having agreed to cover for the relationship between me and G., she also risked prosecution. She might even lose custody of me, in which case I would be placed in a foster home until I reached the age of majority.

She picked up the phone as soon as it rang, palpably apprehensive. After a few seconds her expression relaxed. "G.'s on his way over, he'll be here in ten minutes, he sounded okay, I think it went well," she said in a single breath.

G. came straight from the police station on the Quai de Gesvres, looking rather amused and pleased with himself at how he'd managed to pull the wool over the eyes of the police inspector and her colleagues. "It all went very well," he crowed as soon as he arrived. "The police assured me it was just a bureaucratic formality. 'We receive hundreds of letters denouncing high-profile people every day, you understand, Monsieur,' the inspector told me." As usual, G. was convinced it was all thanks to his irresistible charm. Which was, indeed, not implausible.

At the police station he was shown the letter that had alerted them. Signed "W., a friend of the girl's mother," it described in minute detail some of our recent activities. The specific showing of a movie we'd been to. The day and time I'd arrived at his apartment, and my return to my mother's apartment two hours later. The detailed account of our debauchery was punctuated by judgments along the lines of, "Have you any idea how shameful this is? He genuinely appears to believe himself above the law," and so on. A classic anonymous letter, a model of its kind, virtually a parody. I was horrified. In one strange detail, the letter made me a year younger than I was, presumably to accentuate the gravity of the facts. It spoke of a "young girl of thirteen called V." Who was it who could have spent so much time spying on us? And then there was this strange signature, like a clue placed there for us to guess the author. Otherwise why the initial?

My mother and G. immediately began wildly speculating. We considered every single one of our friends as the potential author of this poison pen missive. Perhaps it was our neighbor on the second floor, an elderly lady who used to be a literature teacher, and who sometimes used to take me to the Comédie Française on a Wednesday afternoon when we didn't have school. Might she have caught us kissing each other full on the lips on the corner of the street? She would have recognized G. (don't forget, she was a literature teacher), and of course she had lived through the Occupation, when plenty of people shamelessly informed on their neighbors in anonymous letters. But it was the "W" that confused us; it was a bit too modern for her. Georges Perec's *W, or the Memory of Childhood* would definitely not have been included in Madame Latreille's literary pantheon; her references would only have gone up to the end of the nineteenth century.

What about the famous literary critic Jean-Didier Wolfromm? He was probably skilled at literary pastiche, as is often the case with people unable to write in the first person. Or unable to write at all, even though it's their profession. "It has to be him," said G. "Look, it's his initial. And he's a friend of your mother, and he took you under his wing."

It was true, Jean-Didier did occasionally invite me to lunch, and he encouraged me to write, who knows why. "V., you must write," he often used to say to me. "To write, well, perhaps this is going to sound idiotic, but you start by sitting down and then . . . you write. Every day. Without exception."

Every room in his apartment was filled to overflowing with books. I always left with a pile under my arm, copies he'd been sent by the publicity departments of publishing houses. He'd make me a little selection. Give me suggestions. Even though he had a reputation for being ungenerous and vindictive, I liked him enormously. He was terribly funny, often at others' expense, but I really couldn't imagine him doing something like this. Attacking G. was the same as attacking me.

I suppose because my father had now completely abandoned me, Jean-Didier had started keeping a benevolent eye on me. I knew he was lonely. I'd seen the tub in his apartment, violet-stained from his daily permanganate bath to treat a ghastly skin condition: his face and hands were red and inflamed, criss-crossed with light cracks. He had extraordinary hands. They fascinated me; he was so comfortable holding a pen, even though his hands were contorted from polio on top of everything else. Curiously, I wasn't repelled by his physical appearance; I always gave him a warm hug. Behind the suffering and the cruel facade, I knew there was someone kind and generous.

"I'm convinced it's that bastard," G. thundered. "He's always been jealous of me because he's a monster. He cannot stand the fact that it's possible to be both handsome and talented. I've always found him quite repulsive. And I'm sure he fantasizes about sleeping with you."

But wouldn't signing himself "W." make it a bit obvious? He might as well have signed his full name. I tried to defend poor Jean-Didier, even though privately I had to admit that he probably was sufficiently twisted to have thought up such a ruse, if the objective was to have G. thrown into prison.

"Or might it be Denis," G. speculated. Denis was a publisher, yet another friend of my mother.

One evening he'd been invited for dinner at our apartment with some other guests. When G. arrived, he stood up and aggressively confronted him. My mother had to ask him to leave. He didn't need to be asked twice. He was one of the very few people—perhaps the only one—who ever tried to get between G. and me, who expressed his outrage publicly. Might he have written this poison pen letter? It wasn't really his style. Why, having attacked G. to his face, would he employ such underhanded tactics?

"What about my old primary school teacher? She still lives in the neighborhood, and we've stayed close. I've never told her about you, but perhaps she spotted us in the street holding hands. She'd be just the type to throw a fit like that. Or the other publisher, Martial, the one with the office on the ground floor where we live, in the courtyard: he's had a hundred opportunities to spy on us coming and going." We hardly knew him. Was it possible that he was the *friend of the girl's mother*?

My classmates from school? Too young to do something so sophisticated. Not their style.

But what about my father? I hadn't heard from him at all since he'd made that scene at the hospital. A few years earlier he'd been thinking of setting up a private detective agency. Maybe he'd decided to put his plan into operation in order to have his daughter followed? I couldn't help thinking that was a possibility. I concealed from G., and presumably from myself too, that deep down this idea gave me a certain pleasure. After all, isn't a father's role to protect his daughter? At least it would indicate that I still mattered to him. But why use the convoluted means of an anonymous letter, rather than simply going straight to the Juvenile Squad? Absurd. No, it couldn't be him. But then again, anything was possible. He was terribly unpredictable.

In two hours, we went through all our acquaintances, conjuring up the most unlikely scenarios. By the end of my first council of war, my entire social circle had become suspect. Not a single one of G.'s enemies was suspected of being the author of the letter. Too many details about me. "It has to be one of your friends," G. declared, fixing my mother with an icy glare.

G. was summoned four more times to the Juvenile Squad. The police received a whole series of letters like the first, but increasingly loaded, filled with more and more intrusive details, spread out over several months. G. would have been shown most of them, if not all.

As far as my mother's close friends were concerned, our relationship was an open secret, but beyond those favored few, we were obliged to exercise great caution. We had to be exceedingly discreet. I was beginning to feel like a hunted animal. The sense of being constantly observed gave birth to a sentiment of paranoia, to which was added a persistent feeling of guilt.

I kept my head down when I was in the street, took increasingly convoluted detours on my way to see G. We made sure never to arrive at the same time. He would get there first, and I would turn up half an hour later. We stopped holding hands when we were together. We no longer walked across the Luxembourg Gardens. After the third summons to the prefecture on the Quai de Gesvres, still "merely a formality," according to the police, G. was starting to seem genuinely nervous.

One afternoon I had just left his apartment, his bed, we were both hurrying down the stairs, I was late, and I almost bumped into a young couple who were on their way up. I politely nodded a greeting to them and continued running down the stairs. When they reached G., I heard them address him. "Monsieur M.? We're from the Juvenile Squad." Apparently even the police watch literary programs on the television, because these two clearly recognized him immediately, even though they had never met before. "It is I," he replied, in a voice that was suave and relaxed. "How may I help you?" I was amazed by his composure. I was trembling like a leaf. Should I run out of the building, hide in the stairwell, call out something in his defense, loudly declare my love for him, create a diversion so he could escape? I realized almost immediately that nothing like that would be necessary.

The tone of the conversation was cordial.

"We were hoping to be able to speak to you, Monsieur M."

"Of course, but as it happens, I have a signing at a bookshop. Might you be able to come back another time?"

"Of course, Monsieur M."

G. gestured in my direction, and said, "Would you mind if I just say goodbye to this young student who came to speak to me about my work?" He shook my hand and gave me a slow wink.

"It's only a routine visit," said the woman.

"Ah, so you mean you haven't come to arrest me." Laughter.

"Of course not, Monsieur M. We'll be back tomorrow, if that suits you."

G. didn't need to worry about them conducting a search. His studio no longer bore the slightest trace of my presence in his life. But, if I had understood correctly, we had only just avoided being caught in flagrante delicto.

Why did neither of the police officers pay any attention to me? I was a teenage girl. The letters all talked of a "young girl of thirteen called V." Admittedly I was actually fourteen, and perhaps I looked a little older.

All the same, it's astounding that it didn't even occur to them.

G. TOOK OUT A LONG-TERM RENTAL OF A HOTEL ROOM for a year to escape further visits from the Juvenile Squad (which he called "intimidation"). The hotel he chose was modest but ideally located—not only was it across the road from my school, but it backed onto the brasserie where G. was a regular, with his own napkin ring. A generous benefactor, a great fan of his work, put up the money for this substantial investment. How else would he be able to write, with the cops on his back? Art takes precedence over everything else.

As in his tiny studio near the Luxembourg Gardens, the first thing one saw upon entering the hotel room was an enormous bed that had pride of place in the center of the room. G. spent more time lying down than sitting or standing; his life, like mine, permanently tended toward the bed. I was spending the night more and more often in this hotel room, only going back to my mother's apartment when she insisted.

One day G. was told that he had a nasty fungal infection in his eyes. The initial hypothesis was that it was HIV. We waited a long, stressful week to get the test results. I wasn't afraid; I rather fancied myself a tragic heroine: if it had to be this way, what an honor and a privilege to die for love! This was what I murmured to G. as I wrapped him in my arms. For his part, however, he appeared somewhat less than reassured. One of his friends was dying of the disease, which had attacked his skin and covered it in a horrible kind of leprosy. G. was only too aware of the merciless nature of the virus, the ensuing decline, the inevitability of death. And nothing filled him with more horror than the idea of physical deterioration. His anxiety was palpable in his every gesture.

G. was hospitalized for the raft of tests he needed to be prescribed the appropriate treatment. AIDS was ruled out. One day the phone rang. I was sitting by his bed in his hospital room, so I answered. A distinguished-sounding woman wished to speak to G. I asked who she was, and she replied in a solemn tone of voice, "The president of the Republic is on the line."

Later, I found out that G. kept a letter in his wallet at all times, in which the president waxed lyrical about G.'s prose style and the immense scope of his cultural knowledge.

The letter was G.'s talisman. In case he was ever arrested, he was sure it would have the power to save him.

IN THE END, G.'S STAY IN THE HOSPITAL WAS BRIEF. AFTER having put to bed the rumor that he had AIDS (easier once he knew for sure he didn't), he took to sporting even larger sunglasses, all the time, and carrying a cane. I began to understand the game he was playing. He loved to dramatize his situation, look for sympathy. Every episode in his life was an opportunity to be instrumentalized.

For the launch of his new book, G. was invited onto the most celebrated books program on television, a mecca for authors. He invited me to go with him.

In the taxi taking us to the television studio, my nose pressed to the window, my distracted glance tracked the century-old facades as they unspooled in the glow of the streetlamps: monuments, trees, passersby, lovers. It was dusk. G. was, as usual, wearing dark glasses. But behind the opaque lenses I could sense his hostile eyes on me.

"What made you decide to put on makeup?" he said finally.

"I . . . I don't know . . . this evening, it's such a special occasion, I wanted to look pretty, for you, to make you happy—"

"And what makes you think that I want to see you looking like a painted lady? You want to look like a 'grown-up,' is that it?"

"G., no, I just wanted to look nice for you, that's all—"

"But I like you to look natural, don't you understand? You don't need to do that. I don't like you like that."

I swallowed my tears, humiliated in front of the driver, who must have thought my father was quite right to tell me off like that. All tarted up, at my age! To go where, again?

Everything was ruined. The evening was going to be a disaster. My mascara had run and now I really did look terrible. I would be introduced to new people, adults who'd look all knowing when they saw me on G.'s arm; I'd have to smile to make him look good, like I did every time he introduced me to his friends. And all the while I felt like slitting my wrists there and then; he'd broken my heart saying I was no longer to his taste.

An hour later, in the studio where the recording was to take place—after we'd kissed and made up, after he'd covered me in kisses and called me his "beloved child," his "beautiful schoolgirl"—I took my place in the audience, overflowing with pride.

Three years later, in 1990, G. was invited back onto the same program, called *Apostrophes*. This time he was called out. I watched part of it several years later on the internet. This episode is rather better known than the one I saw live, because this time G. had not been invited to talk about his inoffensive philosophical dictionary, but the latest volume of his diaries.

In an extract that can still be seen online, the celebrity presenter of the program reels off a list of G.'s conquests, teasing him, in a tone of mild disapproval, about "the stable of young lovers" G. boasts about in his diary.

As the camera cuts away, you see the other guests laughing, not even pretending to disapprove, as the presenter, all fired up now, remarks wryly: "You are, it must be said, something of a connoisseur of teenage girls."

It's all very lighthearted up to that point. Knowing laughter, G.'s face flushed with false modesty.

Suddenly one of the guests lashes out, destroying this delightful harmony and unceremoniously launching a full-frontal attack. Her name is Denise Bombardier. She's a Canadian writer. She says she's scandalized by the presence of such a vile person on a French television channel, a pervert known for defending pedophilia. Citing the age of the best-known of G.M.'s mistresses ("Fourteen!"), she adds that in her country such behavior would be unimaginable, that Canadians are far more progressive when it comes to children's rights. And how do the girls he describes in his books get on with their lives afterward? Has anyone given a thought to them?

G. appears taken aback by her attack, but his response is instantaneous. Coldly furious, he corrects her: "There is not a single fourteen-year-old girl among them; a few are two or three years older, which is absolutely the appropriate age to discover love." (She can't argue, he knows his criminal code.) Then he suggests that she is fortunate to have come across a man as polite and well-mannered as he, who will not stoop to her level of abuse, before finishing up by saying—as he waves his hands around in that feminine way he has that's meant to make him seem quite unthreatening—that not a single one of the young ladies has ever complained about her relationship with him.

Game over. The famous male writer has beaten the virago, who is dismissed as a sex-starved harridan, jealous of the happiness of young women so much more fulfilled than she.

If G. had suffered such an attack in my presence on the evening when I was listening in silence in the audience, how might I have reacted? Would I instinctively have come to his defense? After the recording, would I have tried to explain to this woman that she was wrong, and that no, I was not there against my will? Would I have understood that it was I, hidden among the other spectators, or another young woman like me, whom this woman was trying to protect?

But on that first occasion there was no altercation, no false note to disturb the great event. G.'s book was too high-minded; it didn't lend itself to that. A concert of congratulations, then a drink backstage. G. introduced me to everyone, as was his wont, with undisguised pride. Another nice way of confirming the truth of what he wrote. Adolescent girls were an integral part of his life. And no one appeared in the least bit shocked or embarrassed by the contrast between G. and my plump, girlish cheeks, bare of makeup and any signs of age.

With hindsight, I realize how much courage the Canadian writer must have mustered in order to stand up alone against the complacency of an entire era. Today, time has done its work, and this clip from *Apostrophes* has become what's known as a television "moment."

It's been a long time since G. has been invited onto a book program to flaunt his schoolgirl conquests.

FIRST THERE WERE THE ANONYMOUS LETTERS OF DENUNciation, then the fear that we both had AIDS: successive threats that crystallized our love for each other. We'd have to hide, disappear, flee the intrusive glances of witnesses, jealous people; I'd have to scream across a courtroom, as they handcuffed my beloved, that I loved him more than anything. We would die in each other's arms, our skin covered in sores, stretched tight over our bones, but with a single heart that beat solely for one another . . . Life with G. was more than ever beginning to resemble a novel. Would it have a tragic ending?

Somewhere, surely, there was a path to follow, or to locate. That's what Taoists and Buddhists believe. They call it the "middle way." The right word, the perfect gesture, the irrefutable feeling of being in the right place at the right time. Where the naked truth lies, in a way.

When you're fourteen, it's not normal for a fifty-year-old man to wait for you outside your school. It's not normal to live with him in a hotel, to find yourself in his bed at teatime with his penis in your mouth. I was aware of all that; I may have been only fourteen, but I wasn't completely lacking in common sense. In a way I constructed my new identity out of this very abnormality.

On the other hand, I instinctively understood that the fact that no one ever expressed surprise at the situation meant the world around me was out of kilter.

And when, later on, the different therapists I saw did all they could to explain to me that I'd been the victim of a sexual predator, even then it seemed to me that this wasn't the "middle way" either. That this wasn't quite *right*.

I wasn't yet done with ambivalence.

Part Four

RELEASE

Unless it can be proven to me . . . that, in the infinite run, it does not matter a jot that a North American girl-child named Dolores Haze had been deprived of her childhood by a maniac, unless this can be proven (and if it can, life is a joke) I see nothing for the treatment of my misery but the melancholy and very local palliative of articulate art.

—Vladimir Nabokov, *Lolita*

G. WAS WRITING DAY AND NIGHT. HIS PUBLISHER WAS EXpecting the delivery of the manuscript by the end of the month. It was a stage I'd learned to recognize. This was the second book he was preparing for publication since we'd met the previous year. From the bed, I observed the angular line of his shoulders, bowed over the little typewriter salvaged from the studio we'd run away from. His back, naked and perfectly straight. The fine musculature, the narrow waist wrapped in a towel. I now knew that this slender body came at a price. Rather a high price, in fact. Twice a year, G. went to a specialist Swiss clinic where he ate only salad and grains, and where alcohol and tobacco were forbidden. He came back each time looking five years younger.

Such vanity didn't quite fit with the image I had of a man of letters. Yet it was this body, so smooth and hairless, so slim and lithe, so blond and firm, that I had fallen in love with. But I would have preferred not to know the secrets of its preservation.

In a similar register, I discovered that G. had a terrible phobia of any kind of physical blight. One day in the shower I noticed my chest and arms were covered in red welts. Naked and dripping, I rushed out of the bathroom to show him the marks. But when he saw the rash on my body, he looked utterly horrified, shielded his eyes with one hand, and said, without looking at me:

"Seriously, why are you showing me that? Are you trying to turn me off you completely or what?"

Another time, I was sitting on the bed at the end of the school day, staring at my shoes and crying. There was dead silence in the room. I'd made the mistake of mentioning the name of a classmate who'd invited me to a concert.

"What kind of concert?"

"The Cure. It's New Wave. I was so embarrassed! Everyone knew who they were except me."

"The what?"

"The Cure."

"Would you like to explain what you plan to do at a New Wave concert? Apart from smoking joints while you jiggle your head up and down like a retard? And what's this guy doing inviting you? Is he hoping to grope you between songs, or even worse, corner you in the dark and kiss you? I hope you said no, at least."

As I approached my fifteenth birthday, G. had taken it into his head to control every area of my life. He basically appointed himself my moral guardian. I had to eat less chocolate so I didn't get acne. Watch my figure, in general. Stop smoking (I smoked like a chimney).

Nor was my spiritual health to be overlooked. Every evening he made me read the New Testament, after which he would test me to see if I had understood the meaning of Christ's message in each parable. He was astonished at the extent of my ignorance. I was an atheist, I hadn't been baptized, I was the daughter of a feminist of the May '68 generation, and I was rather mutinous regarding the treatment of women in the text that overall I found not only misogynistic but also repetitive and obscure. But fundamentally I was not displeased with this introduction. The Bible is, after all, a literary text without equal. "No," G. objected when I said this, "it is the book from which all others flow." Between embraces, he also taught me to do the Hail Mary in French and Russian. I had to know the prayer by heart and recite it to myself at night before going to sleep.

But good Lord, what was he afraid of? That the two of us were going to hell?

"Church is for sinners," was his response.

G. WENT TO SWITZERLAND FOR TWO WEEKS FOR HIS REjuvenation cure. He left me the keys to the hotel room as well as to his studio near the Luxembourg Gardens. I was welcome to go there if I wanted to. One evening I violated the taboo and began to read the forbidden books. In one go, like a sleepwalker. I didn't go outside for two days.

The pornography of certain passages, barely veiled by his cultural references and elegant prose style, made me retch. I stopped at one particular paragraph, in which G. described setting out on a quest for "young asses" on a trip to Manila. "Young boys aged eleven or twelve that I bring to my bed are a rare spice," he wrote a little further on.

I thought about his readers. I imagined drooling, physically repulsive old men, transfixed by these descriptions of prepubescent bodies. Did being the heroine of one of G.'s novels mean that I too would become the medium for the masturbatory practices of his pedophile readers?

If G. was indeed a pervert, as he had so often been depicted to me—the sleazy creep who, for the price of an airline ticket to the Philippines, gifted himself an orgy with the bodies of eleven-year-old boys, then justified it with the purchase of a schoolbag—did that make me a monster too?

I immediately tried to suppress this idea. But the poison had found its way in, and now it was beginning to spread.

8:20 A.M. FOR THE THIRD WEEK IN A ROW, I FAILED TO GO into school. I got up, took a shower, got dressed, gulped down my tea, pulled on my backpack, and ran down the staircase in my mother's building. (G. was still away.) It was fine down to the courtyard. But as soon as I went out into the street, things got bad. I was afraid of people's glances, afraid of bumping into someone I knew, someone I might have to speak to. A neighbor, a shopkeeper, a classmate. I clung to the walls, took ridiculous detours along the least populated streets. Each time I caught sight of my reflection in a shop window, my body stiffened, and I found it almost impossible to move it again.

But today I felt resolute, determined, strong. This time I wasn't going to give in to panic. Then that sight as I entered the school building: guards lurking in the shadows, checking all the students' IDs, dozens of backpacks knocking into each other as the kids rushed toward the noisy, messy hive that was the central schoolyard. A teeming, hostile swarm, impossible to avoid. I turned right around and headed down the street in the other direction, toward the market, gasping, my heart thumping, sweating as if I'd committed a crime. Guilty and defenseless.

I took refuge in a local bistro, which was where I spent my time when I wasn't at the hotel. I could spend hours there and no one would bother me. The waiter was always very discreet. He would watch me blackening my journal or reading quietly in the unlikely company of some of the regulars at the bar. He was never anything but tactful. Never asked me why I wasn't in school. Never insisted that I consume more than a single cup of coffee and a glass of water, even if I sat there for three hours in the chilly, anonymous room, where you could sometimes hear the sound of the pinball machine over the clinking of glasses and coffee cups.

I tried to catch my breath. Forced myself to focus. Breathe. Think. Make a decision. I tried to piece together a few sentences in my notebook. But nothing came. Honestly, you couldn't make it up—to be living with a writer and not have the slightest inspiration.

It was 8:35. Three streets away, the bell rang. The students went up the stairs, sat down in pairs, took out their schoolbooks and pencil cases. The teacher entered the classroom. Everyone stopped talking as he took attendance. When he got to the end of the alphabet, he said my name without even bothering to raise his eyes to the back of the class. "Absent, as usual," he said, in a bored tone of voice.

AFTER G.'S RETURN FROM SWITZERLAND, RAGING HARPIES began turning up at all hours outside his room at the hotel. We would hear them weeping in the corridor. Sometimes a girl might slip a note under the doormat. One evening he went out to talk to one of them, closing the door behind him so that I couldn't eavesdrop on their conversation. Shouting and crying, then strangled sobs and whispers. "Everything's going to be okay," he managed to reason with the Valkyrie, who turned and raced back down the stairs.

When I asked G. for an explanation, he pretended they were fans who had followed him down the street, or that they'd somehow managed to obtain his address, mostly through his publisher (a convenient scapegoat), who apparently was insufficiently concerned about his peace of mind.

Then he told me he was going away again, this time to Brussels, where he had been invited to do an event at a bookshop and to speak at a literary festival. I'd be on my own at the hotel again. But a couple of days later, on Saturday, I was walking down the street with a girlfriend when I saw him, arm in arm with a girl on the opposite sidewalk. Like an automaton, I turned on my heels, trying to wipe the image from my mind. It was impossible. G. was in Belgium, he'd sworn to me he was.

I MET G. WHEN I WAS THIRTEEN. WE BECAME LOVERS WHEN I was fourteen. Now I was fifteen and I had no means of comparison, since I had never known any other man. And yet it wasn't long before I became aware of the repetitive nature of our sexual relationship, the difficulties G. had in maintaining his erection, the laborious subterfuges he used to obtain it (frenetically masturbating when I turned over), the increasingly mechanical nature of our lovemaking, the boredom I was beginning to feel, the fear of letting slip anything that might be construed as criticism, the almost insurmountable difficulty of indicating any desire that would not only break our routine but might actually enhance my pleasure. Since I had read the forbidden books, the ones in which he flaunted his collection of mistresses and detailed his trips to Manila, something tacky and sordid now tarnished these intimate episodes in which I could no longer discern the slightest trace of love. I felt degraded and more alone than ever.

And yet, apparently, our love was unique and sublime. He repeated it so often, I ended up believing in its transcendence.

Stockholm syndrome is not just a theory. Why shouldn't a fourteen-year-old girl be in love with a man thirty-six years her senior? I turned this question over in my mind a hundred times, without realizing it was the wrong one. It wasn't my attraction to him that needed to be interrogated, but his to me.

The situation would have been very different if at the same age I'd fallen madly in love with a fifty-year-old man, who, having had several relationships with women his own age, and in spite of knowing it was morally questionable, had succumbed to my youth, fallen madly in love, and yielded just this once to his love for a teenage girl. In that case, I admit, our extraordinary passion might have been *sublime*, if I'd been the one to push him to break the law for love—if not for the fact that G. had repeated the same story a hundred times already. It might indeed have been unique and infinitely romantic if I could have been sure of being the first and the last—if I had, in short, been the exception in his love life. If that had been the case, how could anyone fail to pardon his transgression? Love has no age limit. That was not the issue.

In reality, in the context of G.'s life, I now knew that his desire for me had been repeated an infinite number of times, was pathetically banal, and revealed a neurosis that took the form of an uncontrollable addiction. I might have been the youngest of his Parisian conquests, but his books were peopled with other Lolitas who were fifteen (barely a year older; it hardly made much of a difference), and if he had been living in a country that was less vigilant about protecting minors, my fourteen years wouldn't have been worth a mention next to an eleven-year-old boy with almond-shaped eyes.

G. was not like other men. He boasted of only having had sexual relations with girls who were virgins or boys who had barely reached puberty, then recounted these stories in his books. This was precisely what he was doing when he took possession of my youth for his sexual and literary ends. Every day, thanks to me, he satisfied a passion frowned upon by the law, and prepared to brandish this victory triumphantly in his new novel.

No, this man was not driven by the best intentions. This man was not a good man. He was precisely what we had learned to fear when we were children: an ogre.

Our affair was a dream so powerful that nothing, not a single one of the few warnings I received from those around me, was enough to awaken me. It was the most perverse nightmare. A violence that had no name.

THE SPELL WAS BEGINNING TO LIFT. IT WAS ABOUT TIME. But no Prince Charming came to my aid to slash through the jungle of creepers that bound me to this kingdom of darkness. Every day I awoke to a new reality. A reality that I was still unable to accept in its entirety, for it risked tearing me apart.

But in front of G., I no longer bothered to hide my qualms. What I had found out about him, what he had tried to hide from me up till then, appalled me. I tried to understand. What pleasure did he get from picking up kids in Manila? And why this need to be sleeping with ten girls at once, as he boasted in his diaries? Who was he, really?

When I tried to get an answer, he parried with an attack, calling me an insufferable pedant.

"Who do you think you are, with all your questions? A modern version of the Inquisition? Have you become a feminist all of a sudden? That's the last thing I need!"

From then on, G. assailed me every day with the same mantra:

"You're mad. You don't know how to live in the present, just like every other woman. No woman is capable of savoring the moment, it's as though it's in your genes. You're all chronically unsatisfied, forever imprisoned by your hysteria."

And just like that, there they lay, on the garbage heap of history, all those tender words, all those *my darling childs, my beautiful schoolgirls.*

"In case you've forgotten, I'm only fifteen, as you are perfectly well aware, so not quite yet what one would call a 'woman'! Anyway, what do you know about women? Once they're over eighteen, you're no longer remotely interested in them!"

But I was no match for him when it came to verbal sparring. I was too young, too inexperienced. When I confronted him, the writer and intellectual, I found myself cruelly lacking the necessary vocabulary. I wasn't familiar with the terms "narcissistic pervert" and "sexual predator." I didn't know there was such a thing as a person for whom the Other does not exist. I still believed that violence was only ever physical. And G. manipulated language like others manipulate swords. With the simplest expression he could deal me a fatal blow that would destroy me. It was impossible to do battle with him on equal terms.

Nonetheless, I was old enough to discern the hypocrisy of the situation and recognize that every oath of fidelity, every promise he made to leave me with the most marvelous memories, was just one more lie in the service of his books and his sexual desires. I surprised myself with how much I hated him for trapping me inside the fiction that was being written, constantly, in book after book, in which he always gave himself the best role: a fantasy bolted to his ego, which he then displayed in public. I couldn't bear the way he made a religion out of dissimulation and lies and used his vocation as a writer as an alibi to justify his addiction. I was no longer taken in by his games.

He, meanwhile, began to resent even the most offhand remark I made. His diary became my worst enemy, the means by which G. filtered our love affair, transforming it into an unhealthy and entirely one-sided passion that I had single-handedly crafted. At the first hint of a reproach, he would rush to uncap his pen: "You shall see what you shall see, my pretty one! What a portrait I'm going to sketch of you in my little black book!"

Because I was turning against him, because it no longer gave me any joy to slip under the sheets between lessons, he had to get rid of me. With the power of the written word, he turned his "little V." into an unstable teenage girl eaten up with jealousy. He said whatever he wanted; I was just a character now, living on borrowed time, like every other girl who'd come before me. It wouldn't be long before he erased me completely from the pages of his wretched diary. For his readers, it was merely a story, words. For me, it was the beginning of a breakdown.

But what is the life of an anonymous adolescent worth compared to a work of literature written by a superior being?

The fairy tale was over, the spell was broken, and Prince Charming had revealed his true face.

ONE AFTERNOON AFTER SCHOOL I WALKED THROUGH THE door into his room in the hotel. It was empty; G. was shaving in the bathroom. I put my schoolbag on a chair and sat down on the mattress. One of his black notebooks had been casually tossed onto the bed. It was open at the page where G. had scrawled a few lines in his signature turquoise ink: "4:30 p.m. Picked up Nathalie from school. When she caught sight of me on the sidewalk on the other side of the street, her face lit up. Surrounded by all these other young people, she looked as radiant as an angel . . . We spent a delicious, divine time together. She is extraordinarily passionate. I wouldn't be surprised if this young girl were to end up having a more significant future in these diaries."

The words detached themselves from the page in a swarm, like a crowd of demons, as my whole world collapsed around me. The furniture in the bedroom became a heap of smoking ruins; cinders floated in the air that I could no longer breathe.

G. came out of the bathroom. He found me in tears, my eyes bloodshot, gesturing in disbelief at the open notebook. He turned pale, then flew into a rage and exploded.

"What? How dare you make a scene! How dare you disturb

my work! I'm in the middle of writing a novel! Can you imagine for a moment the pressure I'm under? Can you even remotely conceive of the energy and concentration required? You have no idea what it is to be an artist, a creator! It's true I don't have to clock in at a factory every day, but the agony I go through when I am writing, you haven't the slightest idea what it's like! What you've just read is just the outline of a future novel—it has nothing to do with us, nothing to do with you."

This lie was the last straw. I might have only just turned fifteen, but I couldn't help seeing what he said as an insult to my intelligence, a wholehearted rejection of me as a person. This betrayal of all his fine promises, this revelation of his true nature, winded me like a punch in the gut. There was nothing left between us. I'd been cheated, tricked, abandoned to my fate. And I only had myself to blame. I hoisted a leg over the window balustrade and prepared to jump. He pulled me back in at the last moment.

I slammed the door as I left.

I'D ALWAYS HAD A PROPENSITY FOR WANDERING, AND A perplexing fascination for the local drifters I stopped to chat with at the slightest opportunity. That afternoon I roamed the neighborhood in a daze for hours, looking for some kindred spirit, a human being to talk to. Beneath a bridge I sat down alongside a down-and-out and dissolved into tears. The old man barely raised an eyebrow and mumbled some words in a language I didn't recognize. We sat for a while in silence, watching the barges as they floated by. Then I stood up and went on my way, not heading in any particular direction.

Almost mechanically, I eventually found myself in front of an elegant apartment building where one of G's friends lived—Emil Cioran, a Romanian-born philosopher whom he had introduced to me at the beginning of our relationship as his mentor.

I was filthy, my hair was a mess, my face smudged with dirt from the hours I'd spent sitting on the ground in the neighborhood whose every bookshop, every crack in the sidewalk, every tree reminded me of G. I pushed open the heavy door of the building. Trembling, dirt beneath my fingernails, sweating, I must have looked like a vagabond who'd just given birth behind a bush. Tiptoeing, my heart thumping, I made my way up the carpeted staircase and rang the bell, my face burning as I held back tears. A diminutive middle-aged woman opened the door. She looked at me with a guarded expression. I said I was sorry to disturb, but I'd like to see her husband if he was home; all of a sudden Emil's wife's expression turned to horror as she took in my disheveled appearance. "Emil, it's V., G.'s friend!" she shouted toward the other end of the apartment, then bustled down a corridor that led to the kitchen, and from the metallic sounds I guessed she was putting on the kettle to make a cup of tea.

Cioran came into the room, one eyebrow raised, a discreet but eloquent indication of his surprise, and invited me to sit down. That was all it took for me to burst into tears. I wept like a baby howling for its mother, pathetically using my sleeve to try to wipe the snot from my nose. Cioran handed me an embroidered handkerchief.

The blind confidence that had led me to him was predicated on a single thing: his resemblance to my grandfather, who was also born in Eastern Europe. He had the same white hair with a receding hairline, combed toward the back of the head, the same piercing blue eyes, the same hooked nose and accent that could be cut with a knife (*"Tzitrón? Tchocoláte?"* as he poured the tea).

I'd never managed to finish any of his books, even though they're extremely short, composed as they are only of aphorisms. He was known as a "nihilist." And, it turned out, in this regard he did not disappoint.

"Emil, I can't bear it any longer," I said, hiccupping between sobs. "He tells me I'm crazy, and I shall end up going crazy if he carries on like this. His lies, the way he just disappears, all the girls who keep turning up at the hotel. I feel like a prisoner. I've got no one else to talk to. He's alienated me from my friends, my family . . ."

"V.," he interrupted me, in a very serious tone of voice. "G. is an artist, a great writer, and one day the world will recognize him as such. Or perhaps not, who knows? If you love him, you must accept who he is. G. will never change. It is an immense honor to have been chosen by him. Your role is to accompany him on the path of creation, and to bow to his impulses. I know he adores you. But too often women do not understand an artist's needs. Did you know that Tolstoy's wife spent her days typing out the manuscripts that her husband wrote in longhand, tirelessly correcting every single mistake? She was utterly self-sacrificing and self-effacing, which is precisely the kind of devotion that every artist's wife owes the man she loves."

"But, Emil, he never stops lying to me."

"But literature is all about lying, my dear young friend! Didn't you realize?"

I couldn't believe what I was hearing. Was this really him, the great philosopher, the wise man, uttering these words? Was he, the supreme intellectual authority, really asking a fifteen-year-old girl to put her life on hold for the sake of an old pervert? Telling her to zip it, once and for all? I couldn't take my eyes off Cioran's wife's chubby little fingers gripping the handle of the teapot. I managed to restrain myself from releasing the flood of invective burning my lips. All dolled up, her blue-tinted hair matching her blouse, silently nodding at her husband's every word. Once upon a time she'd been a successful actress. At some point she stopped making films. No need to ask when that was. The only practical observation that Emil deigned to offer me—more enlightening than I realized at the time—was that G. would never change.

SOMETIMES AFTER SCHOOL I USED TO BABYSIT A LITTLE boy, the son of one of my mother's neighbors. I helped him with his homework, gave him a bath, made his supper, played with him a bit, then put him to bed. On evenings when his mother was going out for dinner, a young man took over from me.

Youri was a twenty-two-year-old law student who played the saxophone and worked part-time to pay for his studies. Coincidentally—or not—he also had Russian origins, through his father. At first we merely crossed paths. We'd greet each other, exchange a few words, to start with, anyway. But after a few weeks, I began staying a little longer before going home. We were growing fond of each other.

One evening the two of us were leaning on the windowsill looking out as it grew dark. Youri asked me if I had a boyfriend, and I found myself confiding in him, timidly at first, and then eventually divulging the details of my situation. Again, I spoke of myself as if I were a prisoner. At the age of fifteen I was trapped in a labyrinth, unable to get back on track, my daily life an endless round of arguments followed by pillow talk, our time in bed the only moment I still felt loved. It drove me crazy, on the rare occasions I went into school, to compare myself to my classmates, who went home to listen to their Étienne Daho and Depeche Mode records and eat bowls of cereal, while I was satisfying the sexual urges of a man who was older than my father, because my fear of being abandoned was stronger than reason, and I persisted in believing that this abnormal situation made me interesting.

I looked up at Youri. His face was puce with anger and his features were twisted into a violent expression that I wouldn't have imagined him capable of. He took my hand with an unexpected gentleness and stroked my cheek. "Do you not realize how much this bastard is exploiting and hurting you? You're not the one to blame, he is! You're not crazy and you're not a prisoner. You just have to get your confidence back and leave him."

G. COULD SEE I WAS SLIPPING AWAY FROM HIM. IT WAS obviously intolerable for him to feel that I was no longer under his thumb, although I had said nothing to him about my conversations with Youri. For the first time, G. suggested that I go with him to the Philippines. He wanted to prove to me that the country was nothing like the devil's lair that he described in his books. Most of all he wanted the two of us to go somewhere far away, to the other side of the world, *anywhere out of the world*. To get close to each other again, to love each other like the very first time. I was paralyzed. The thought of agreeing terrified me, and yet I had an irrepressible longing, an absurd hope, that I would see my nightmare dissipate, would discover that the sickening descriptions in some of his books were just phantasmagoria, provocations, narcissistic boasts. That in fact there was no child sex trade in Manila. That there never had been. Deep down I knew it wasn't true, deep down I knew that it would be crazy to go there with him. Would he expect me to share our bed with an eleven-year-old boy? In any case, my mother, to whom he had boldly made his absurd request, had the presence of mind to refuse point-blank. Since

I was a minor, I couldn't leave the country without her permission. Her refusal took a great weight off my shoulders.

For a while now G. had been insisting on the gap between fiction and reality, between his writing and his real life, which he claimed I was unable to grasp. He was always trying to throw me off the scent, to thwart the sixth sense I had that enabled me to detect his lies. Gradually I was discovering the extent of his talent as a manipulator, the mountain of falsehoods he had built up between us. It was an extraordinary strategy, the way he calculated every minute detail. His entire intellect revolved around satisfying his desires and then transposing them into one of his books. Every single act was guided by these two motives: writing and coming.

AN UNSETTLING IDEA HAD BEGUN TO GERMINATE IN MY mind. An idea that was made even more unbearable by the fact that it was entirely plausible; indisputably logical, even. Once it had surfaced, it proved hard to shake.

G. was the only person in our social circle whom I'd never suspected of being behind the series of anonymous letters. Yet their frequency and their intrusiveness conferred on the beginnings of our love affair a dangerous, novelistic glamour: we were alone against the world, united in the face of the revulsion of decent, law-abiding people; we'd had to brave the suspicions of the police, submit to their inquisitorial looks, we'd even suspected all my friends and acquaintances, who'd turned into a single enemy, a monster with a thousand pairs of jealous eyes trained upon us. Who other than G. would these letters have benefited? Not only did they bond us to one another better than the hatred between two Sicilian families ever could, but, after having definitively alienated me from every person who might be even vaguely critical of him, G. would be able to recycle them into his next novel, and publish them in their entirety in his diary (which is precisely what he went on to do, as a matter of fact). Of course, it was a risky endeavor. He might have been sent to prison. But even that would have been worth it: what a plot twist, what a coup de théâtre, what material for a book! If he were arrested, he could count on my devotion; he knew I would shout my love for him from the rooftops, I'd shriek at the top of my voice how in a more tolerant country we would be allowed to marry, I'd demand my legal independence from my parents, alert officials and celebrities who would rally around our cause. What a fabulous spectacle it would have made! In fact, as it turned out, the police were rather less suspicious than one might have imagined, and all the decent, law-abiding people returned to their daily lives without worrying unduly about "little V.," and the occasional fits of indignation of those around us gradually faded away. Thinking about it, it seems obvious to me now—though my memory might be playing tricks on me—that it was precisely during this period, when the police, at last, began to leave him alone, that boredom, and the incipient, though initially imperceptible, loss of interest in our relationship, began to worm its way inside him.

ONCE, JUST ONCE, I DARED TO ASK HIM A QUESTION THAT up until then had never even occurred to me. I felt compelled to ask this unwonted question in spite of my youth—unless it was, rather, precisely because of my youth. Once it had occurred to me, it nagged at me insistently, and I held on to it like a life preserver, because it offered me the hope that I might somehow recognize myself a little in G. I had to ask him this question, as sensitive as it was, without lowering my eyes from his, without trembling, without looking away.

We were lying alongside each other in his room in the sleazy hotel, sharing a moment of intimacy and tranquility, without quarreling or griping, tears or doors slamming. Something sad now lodged between us. The knowledge that the end was coming, the exhaustion from constantly hurting each other. G. ran his fingers through my hair. I started to speak.

Had there been an adult during his childhood or adolescence who'd taken the role of his "initiator"? I deliberately avoided using words like "rape," "abuse," or "sexual assault."

To my great surprise, G. admitted that yes, there had been someone, once, when he was thirteen: a man, a friend of the family. There was no affect in this revelation. Not a trace of emotion. And I don't think I'm mistaken in noting that there is no evidence of this memory in any of his books. Yet it is surely an enlightening element of his autobiography. As I had learned at my expense, the aim of G.'s literary process was to distort reality to flatter himself. It was never about revealing even a scrap of truth about himself. Or if it was, it was always cloaked with too much narcissism to lay claim to any genuine honesty. This infinitesimal instant of candor, these unexpected words addressed to me were his unwitting gift to me. I became a person again in my own right, rather than simply the object of his pleasure. I was someone in possession of a little secret about his past, someone who could hear him, perhaps, without judging him. Someone who understood him, perhaps, better than anyone else.

YOURI'S GENTLE PRESENCE, HIS THOUGHTFULNESS, THE very few faithful friends I'd grown apart from over the previous two years with whom I was timidly reviving our friendship, and the longing to dance and laugh with people my own age began to supplant G.'s hold over me. Our emotional bond was coming loose, and the jungle in the depraved kingdom was opening up to a different world where, against all the odds, the sun shone and was just waiting for me to show up for the party to begin. G. went away for a month. He needed to make some progress with his new book. In Manila, there would be no distractions, he swore to me disingenuously. Every day Youri tried to persuade me to leave G., but it was impossible to confront him before he left. What was I afraid of? I vowed to take advantage of his absence by writing to him. Our love affair would end as it had begun: by letter. Deep down inside, I was sure that he was expecting our breakup. That he wanted it, even. A strategist beyond compare, I reminded myself.

But, as things turned out, it was quite the opposite. After he returned from the Philippines, he wrote to tell me how devastated he had been by my letter. He didn't understand. I still loved him: every single word I wrote betrayed my real feelings. How could I draw a line under our love affair, the most beautiful, the purest love story that had ever been? He pestered me by phone, in letters, began following me down the street again. He was outraged by my decision to leave him. The only person he loved was me. There was no other girl in his life. As for the Philippines, he swore blind he had behaved with irreproachable chastity. But that wasn't the problem now. I didn't care about him and his escapades anymore. It was my redemption I was seeking, not his.

When I told my mother I had left G., she was momentarily struck dumb, then she said, sadly, "Poor thing, are you sure? He adores you!"

Part Five

THE IMPRINT

It is curious that a first love, if by the frail state in which it leaves our heart it opens the way to our subsequent loves, does not at least provide us, in view of the identity of symptoms and sufferings, with the means of curing them.

—Marcel Proust, *The Captive*

G. GREW TIRED OF FIGHTING, GAVE UP PURSUING ME WITH his letters, and stopped calling my mother, whom he had been imploring day and night to stop me from severing contact with him.

Youri took his place in my life. He gave me the courage to leave G. and to resist all his frantic attempts to make me go back on my decision. I turned sixteen and moved in with Youri, who still shared a small apartment with his mother. My own mother didn't argue. We weren't on very good terms. I frequently reproached her for having failed to protect me. She would answer that my resentment was unjustified; all she'd done was respect my desires and let me live my life as I wished.

"You're the one who was sleeping with him and I'm the one who's supposed to apologize?" she said to me one day.

"So the fact that I hardly ever go to school anymore, the number of times I've nearly been expelled, it was a symptom of something, no? You might have noticed that my life hasn't exactly been a bed of roses."

But the conversation was impossible. Logically, the fact that she had accepted my relationship with G. meant that she considered me already an adult. Which meant that my choices were entirely my own.

Now all I wanted was to have a normal life, the life of someone my own age: under no circumstances to rock the boat, to be like everyone else. Now things ought to be easier. I was in high school. I was going to start going to school again. I was determined not to draw sidelong glances from certain students; I'd ignore the rumors that were starting to circulate among the teachers. "That new girl, apparently G.M. used to come and pick her up every day after class. I know some of the teachers at her old school—you know she was at Prévert—they told me. Can you imagine? And her parents just turned a blind eye!" One day I was having a coffee at the counter of the bistro where all the students used to hang out between classes. A teacher came and sat down beside me. He told me I was the subject of discussion in the teachers' lounge.

"You're the girl who was dating G.M., aren't you? I've read all his books. I'm a big fan."

It would have been extremely satisfying to turn around and answer, "So you're a disgusting pervert, right?" But now I had to make a good impression. I smiled politely, paid for my coffee, and left, trying to ignore the lewd way he stared at my breasts.

It's not easy to regain your virginity.

Another day, a man stopped me on a side street, not far from my school. He knew my name. Told me he'd seen me several times in the neighborhood with G. a few months earlier. Unleashed a torrent of obscenities, lavish details about everything I presumably knew how to do in bed now, thanks to G. A heroine straight out of Sade!

Nothing excites these old men more than the thought of a completely depraved teenage girl.

I ran. I was crying by the time I got to school.

Youri did what he could to stave off my bouts of despair, which he was beginning to find oppressive, not least because he thought they were unjustified. "Come on, please, you're young, your whole life is ahead of you. Smile!" Except that I was nothing but a ball of rage exhausting myself by acting like everything was fine, trying to pull the wool over everyone's eyes. I did everything I could to suppress this anger, concealing it by turning it back on myself. The guilty party was me. I was the dropout, the slut, the good-time girl, the pedophile's accomplice, the young woman whose besotted letters served as a kind of approval for the charter flights to Manila carrying perverts who masturbated over photos of boy scouts. And when I could no longer mask my distress, I sank into a depression, where all I wanted was to disappear from the face of the earth.

Only Youri, perhaps, could see it. He adored me, with the youthful ardor of a twenty-two-year-old, and what he loved more than anything was making love. Who could blame him?

When it came to sex, I oscillated between feeling all-powerful and completely apathetic. Sometimes I was filled with a feeling of intoxication—all this power! How easy it was to make a man happy. And then suddenly, at the point of orgasm, I'd dissolve into tears for no apparent reason. Too much happiness, was all I could tell him when he showed concern at my sobs. For entire days I couldn't bear for him to touch me. And then the infernal cycle would begin again. I would recall my mission in life: pleasuring men. That was my condition, my status. And so I would offer my services anew, with renewed zeal and a simulated conviction that I even managed to convince myself was real. I faked it. Faked enjoying sex, faked my pleasure, faked knowing what the point of it all was. Deep down I was ashamed of being able to do it all so instinctively, when others had barely experienced their first kiss. I knew perfectly well I'd skipped a stage. I'd gone too fast, too early, with the wrong person. I wished I'd experienced all those moments of intimacy for the first time with Youri. I wished he had been my initiator, my first lover.

Yet I didn't dare admit it. I didn't have enough confidence in myself, or in him.

And more than anything, I couldn't tell him that the image I couldn't get out of my head whenever we made love was G.

Yet G. had promised to bequeath me the most wonderful memories.

For years, however tender and considerate the boys with whom I attempted an uncomplicated sexual relationship, I found myself unable to get back to the point Julien and I had reached—the moment of innocent discovery and shared pleasure between two equal beings.

Later, with a little more maturity and courage, I opted for a different strategy: to tell the entire truth, admit that I felt like a doll lacking all desire who had no idea how her own body worked, who had learned only one thing: how to be an instrument for other people's games.

Every time, this revelation brought the relationship to an end. No one wants a broken toy.

IN 1974, TWELVE YEARS BEFORE WE MET, G. PUBLISHED AN essay entitled *Under Sixteen*, a manifesto of sorts calling for the sexual liberation of minors, which simultaneously caused a scandal and made him famous. Though the scandal was extremely damaging, it endowed G.'s work with an inflammatory dimension that increased interest in his writing in general. While his friends thought it would be social suicide, it turned out that on the contrary, the book gave his literary career a boost, bringing him to the notice of a broader public.

I hadn't read it and I didn't grasp its import until many years after our relationship ended.

In the essay, G. championed the theory that the sexual initiation of children is a positive act that should be encouraged by society. The practice was widespread in antiquity, evidence of the ancients' recognition of the right of adolescents to their freedom of choice and desire.

"The very young are tempting. They are also tempted. I have never stolen so much as a kiss or a caress by coercion or force," he writes.

He must have forgotten the times when those kisses and

caresses were paid for, in countries less punctilious about underage prostitution. If one were to believe the descriptions he jotted down in his black Moleskine notebooks, one might even be persuaded that Filipino children threw themselves at him through sheer greed, the way a child might pounce on a strawberry ice cream. (Unlike all those bourgeois Western children, the children of Manila are liberated.)

In *Under Sixteen* he militates for a complete liberalization of morals, an open-mindedness that would at last authorize an adult not to orgasm *over* an adolescent but *with* an adolescent. What a worthy project. Or the worst kind of sophistry. In the essay, and in the open letter that G. went on to publish three years later, when you look closely at what he says, it becomes clear that he is not defending the interests of adolescents, but those of adults "unjustly" convicted for having had sexual relationships with them.

The role that G. liked to give himself in his books was that of benefactor, responsible for the initiation of young people into the joys of sex; a professional, a veteran; in other words—if one might dare to be so bold—an expert. In reality, this exceptional talent was limited to not making his partner suffer. And where there is neither pain nor coercion, there is no rape. The challenge of the undertaking consists in respecting this golden rule, without exception. Physical violence leaves a memory for a person to react against. It's appalling, but tangible.

Sexual abuse, on the other hand, is insidious and perverse,

and the victim might be barely aware it is happening. No one speaks of "sexual abuse" between adults. Of the abuse of the vulnerable, yes, of an elderly person, for example. *Vulnerability* is precisely that infinitesimal space into which people with the psychological profile of G. can insinuate themselves. It's the element that makes the notion of consent so beside the point. Very often, in the case of sexual abuse or abuse of the vulnerable, one comes across the same denial of reality, the same refusal to consider oneself a victim. And indeed, how is it possible to acknowledge having been abused when it's impossible to deny having consented, having felt desire, for the very adult who was so eager to take advantage of you? For many years I struggled with the very idea of the victim, and was incapable of seeing myself as one.

G. was right about the fact that puberty and adolescence are periods of explosive sensuality: sex is everywhere, you're overflowing with desire, it invades you, it's like a wave, it has to be satisfied straightaway; all that's needed is an encounter with another person to share it with.

But some differences are simply irresolvable. With all the goodwill in the world, an adult is still an adult. And an adult's desire can only ever be a trap for an adolescent. How can both have the same level of understanding of their bodies, their desires? What's more, a vulnerable adolescent is always going to seek love before sexual satisfaction. Sometimes, in exchange for an indication of affection (or the sum of money their family needs), an adolescent will agree to become the object of pleasure, thus renouncing, for a long time to come, the right to be the subject, actor, and master of their own sexuality.

What characterizes sexual predators in general and pedophiles in particular is the refusal to acknowledge the gravity of their acts. They tend to present themselves either as victims (they were seduced by a child, or a female temptress) or as benefactors (who did only *good* to their victims).

In *Lolita*, Nabokov's novel, which I read and reread after I first met G., the reader is, on the contrary, confronted with confusing disclosures. Humbert Humbert pens his confession in the psychiatric hospital where he later dies, not long before his trial. He does not go easy on himself at all.

How lucky Lolita was: at least she obtained this compensation, the unambiguous recognition of her stepfather's guilt, in the voice of the very person who had stolen her childhood. How unfortunate that she was already dead when he made his confession.

Nowadays I often hear it said that a work like Nabokov's, were it to be published today, in our so-called neo-Puritan era, would inevitably encounter censorship. And yet I don't think that *Lolita* is even remotely an apology for pedophilia. Quite the contrary: it's the strongest possible denunciation of it—the most compelling ever written on the subject. I've never believed that Nabokov was a pedophile. Obviously, his persistent interest in such a subversive subject—which he tackled twice, first in *The Enchanter*, in his native Russian, then, several years later, in English, with the iconic *Lolita*, which garnered worldwide success—raised a few suspicions. Nabokov might indeed have struggled against such a predilection. I couldn't possibly know. But despite all of Lolita's subconscious perversity, despite her games of seduction and her starlet's simpering, Nabokov never tried to make Humbert Humbert pass for a benefactor, and still less for a decent person. The tale of his character's passion for young girls, an unrestrained and pathological passion that tortured him throughout his entire life, is, on the contrary, implacably clear-sighted.

In his books, G. comes across as far from contrite or self-questioning. Not a trace of regret or remorse. Reading him, you might imagine he was brought into this world to offer adolescents the fulfillment that a culture of inhibition denied them, to open them up to their desires, reveal their sensuality, develop their capacity to give and to receive.

Such a capacity for self-denial merits a statue in the Luxembourg Gardens.

IT WAS THANKS TO G. THAT I DISCOVERED, AT MY EXPENSE, HOW books can be a snare to trap those one claims to love, how they can become a blunt instrument for betrayal. As if his appearance in my life had not been devastating enough, now he had to document it, falsify it, record it, brand it forever with his crimes.

The panicked reaction among primitive peoples when their image is captured can give rise to amusement. Now I understood better than anyone the feeling of being trapped in a deceptive likeness, a reductive version of oneself, a grotesque, contorted snapshot. To seize the image of the other with such brutality is indeed to steal their soul.

G.'s novels, in which I was supposedly the heroine, appeared in bookshops when I was between the ages of sixteen and twenty-five, at a rhythm that left me no respite. After that came the volume of his diary covering the period of our relationship, including some letters I wrote when I was fourteen; two years later the paperback version of the same book; then a collection of breakup letters, including mine. That's without counting all the newspaper articles and television interviews in which he reveled in saying my first name. Later there would be another volume of the contents of his little black notebooks, in which he returned almost obsessively to the subject of our separation.

Every one of these publications, whatever the context in which I found out about it (there was always some well-intentioned person excited to let me know), bordered on harassment. For everybody else it was the beating of a butterfly's wings on a tranquil lake, but for me it was like an earthquake, an invisible tremor that upended the very foundations of my life, a blade plunged into a wound that had never scarred over, a hundred steps backward in the progress I thought I had made in getting on with my life.

When I read the volume of his diaries that was largely devoted to our breakup, it triggered a terrible panic attack. G. had begun to instrumentalize our relationship by depicting it through the prism that most flattered him. His brainwashing tactics were positively Machiavellian. In his diary he transformed our love affair into the perfect fiction. That of a libertine transformed into a saint, of a rehabilitated pervert, a chronically unfaithful man who got his second chance, a fiction that he wrote but never lived, published after the requisite interval—that is, the period of time necessary for life to be duly dissipated in a novel. I was the betrayer, the woman who had ruined this perfect love, who had destroyed everything by refusing to go along with this transformation. The woman who had not wanted to *believe* in this fiction.

I was stupefied by his refusal to recognize that this love carried within it his own failure, from the first moment, that it had no possible future because the only thing G. was able to love in me was a fugitive, transitory moment: my adolescence.

I read the book in one sitting, in a fugue state, a confused stupor of powerlessness and rage, horrified by his lies and bad faith, by his propensity for self-victimization and the way he shifted responsibility for any blame away from himself. I held my breath as I got to the final pages, as if some invisible force was pressing on my solar plexus and my throat. All the vital energy drained from my body, as though absorbed by the ink of this vile book. I only managed to calm down after a shot of valium.

I also learned that, in spite of my categorical refusal to be in contact with him, G. continued, deviously, to stay informed about what I was up to. Through whom, I don't know. In the pages of his diary he even insinuated that after we had broken up I'd begun hanging out with a junkie, thanks to whom I had ended up in a vortex of the most abject debauchery, just as he had predicted I would when I left him. He, my protector, had done all he could to keep me away from the hazards of youth.

This was how G. justified his role in the lives of the adolescent girls he seduced. He kept them from becoming lost souls, social rejects. All those poor, hapless girls whose lives he had tried, in vain, to save!

No one told me at the time that I could press charges, sue his publisher, that he didn't have the right to publish my letters without my consent, nor to write about the sex life of someone who was a minor at the time of the relationship, making her recognizable, not just by the use of her first name and the initial of her last but with a thousand other little details. For the first time I began to see myself as a victim, though I couldn't put my finger on the word for that hazy feeling of powerlessness. I also had the vague sense that not only had I been used to satisfy his sexual urges during our relationship, but now I was being used to cast a favorable light on him, enabling him, through no efforts of my own, to continue to broadcast his literary propaganda.

After I read the book, I had the profound sense that my life had been ruined before I had even lived it. With a stroke of his pen my history had been erased, carefully wiped away, then revised and rewritten in black and white, and published in an edition of a thousand copies. What link could there be between this paper character, fabricated from beginning to end, and the person I really was? Turning me into a fictional character, when my adult life had barely begun, was a way of preventing me from spreading my wings, of condemning me to remaining trapped in a prison made of words. G. must have known this. But I suppose he simply didn't care.

He had immortalized me; what could I possibly have to complain about?

Writers do not always profit by becoming famous. It would be wrong to imagine they are like other people. They are much, much worse.

They are vampires.

I gave up any literary ambition I'd ever harbored.

I stopped keeping a diary.

I turned my back on books.

I no longer had any interest in writing.

PREDICTABLY, ALL MY EFFORTS TO GET BACK ON THE RIGHT track failed. My anxiety attacks returned with a vengeance. I began skipping school regularly. After two disciplinary hearings, the school principal, a woman who up until that point had only shown me extraordinary kindness, called me into her office.

"I'm sorry, V., but with the best will in the world, I cannot continue to fight in your favor. The teachers have taken against you. Because of your repeated absences, the way you reject their authority, deny them their role." (They weren't wrong: the way I thought about adults was beyond anything they might have imagined.) "On top of everything else, you're setting a bad example for your classmates. Some of the other students are beginning to emulate your behavior. We have to put a stop to this situation."

If I didn't want to be expelled from school, which would have gone into my academic dossier and been bad for my future prospects, she suggested that I leave of my own accord, for "personal reasons." I could sit my baccalaureate examinations as an independent candidate. After all, attending school is not compulsory after the age of sixteen.

"You'll do fine, V. I'm not worried about that at all."

I had no choice. I agreed. I was used to an unconventional lifestyle, without structure or framework. And now I would no longer be constrained by school hours. No matter! I'd spend my final year of high school sitting in cafés and studying via correspondence.

I spent my nights dancing and drinking. I had the occasional unpleasant encounter, of which I have no recollection. I left Youri; I couldn't bear putting him through my depressions anymore. I met another boy, intelligent and gentle, but horribly damaged, someone like me who was silently falling apart, whose sadness could only be chased away by artificial highs. I copied his behavior. Yes, G. was right, I was on the road to perdition. He had made me lose my mind. And I was doing everything I could to stay in character.

IT HAPPENED WITHOUT WARNING, ALMOST FROM ONE DAY to the next. I was walking along an empty street, an unsettling question going around and around in my head, a question that had wormed its way into my mind several days earlier that I couldn't shake off: What proof did I have of my existence? Was I even real? In an attempt to figure this out once and for all, I had stopped eating. What was the point of nourishing myself? My body was made of paper, ink flowed through my veins, my organs didn't exist. I was a fiction. After a few days of fasting, I began to feel the first flutter of a kind of euphoria replacing my hunger. A lightness I had never felt before. I was no longer walking; now I was gliding along the ground, and if I'd flapped my arms, I would surely have flown away. I felt no emptiness, not the slightest stomachache, not even a vague tug of hunger at the sight of an apple or a piece of cheese. I was no longer part of the material world.

And because my body could cope with the absence of food, why would it need to sleep? From dusk to dawn I kept my eyes open. There was nothing to break the continuity between day and night. Until one evening when I went to check in the bathroom mirror that my reflection was still there. Curiously, it was still there, but what was new, and fascinating, was that now I could see right through it.

I was disappearing, evaporating, slipping away. A dreadful sensation, like being ripped from the realm of the living, but in slow motion. As though my soul was leaking through the pores of my skin. I began wandering the streets all through the night, searching for a sign. Some proof of life. Around me, the city, misty and otherworldly, was taking on the sepia hues of an old film. If I raised my eyes, the railings of the public garden in front of which I was standing seemed to be moving on their own, turning like a magic lantern, three or four images a second, like eyelids blinking, slowly and regularly. Something inside me was still in revolt. I wanted to scream: *Is anybody there?*

Two people emerged from the door of an apartment building. They were carrying heavy wreaths of funeral flowers. Their lips were moving, I could hear the sound of their voices addressing me, yet I couldn't make out any intelligible meaning in their words. Just a few seconds earlier I had been thinking that the sight of living beings would help me grasp hold of reality, but this was worse than the immobile landscape of the sleeping city. In the space of a moment, so elusive that I might have dreamed it, I said to them, as if to reassure myself,

"Excuse me, do you have the time?"

"There is no time for the weak," one of them replied, his back bowed by the weight of the wreath, whose luminous colors cast a glow up his arm. But perhaps what he'd actually said was, "There is no time for weeping."

A feeling of overwhelming grief broke over me.

I looked at my hands and I could see right through to the bones, nerves, tendons, flesh, and even cells teeming beneath my skin. Anyone could have seen through my body. I was nothing but a powdery cluster of photons. Everything around me was fake and I was no exception.

A police van appeared around the corner. Two men in uniform got out. One of them came toward me.

"What are you doing here? You've been walking around this garden for the last hour. Are you lost?"

Because I was crying, and because I backed away, frightened, the man turned to his colleague, who rummaged around the front seat of the vehicle and returned with a sandwich in his hand.

"Are you hungry? Here, have this."

I didn't dare move. He opened the back door of the van and said,

"Why don't you get in and warm up?"

He was trying to sound unthreatening, but when he pointed to the two parallel benches in the back, I saw an electric chair, waiting just for me.

How long had it been since I lost all trace of myself? Why did I accumulate so much guilt, to the point of believing that I merited a death sentence? I had no idea. At least that's how it seemed to me when, in the early hours of the morning, I found myself in a gloomy hospital where a bearded professor, who was clearly revered by the junior doctors who were listening to him as if he were the Messiah, was interrogating me about the experience that had led me to this sad shelter for mad, crazed, anorexic, suicidal, desperate people. There was a video camera set up at the back of the room.

"Mademoiselle, you have just experienced a psychotic episode, with a phase of depersonalization," said the bearded man. "Please ignore the camera. I want you to tell me what happened."

"You mean all this is true? I'm not . . . *fiction*?"

IT WAS AS THOUGH I HAD LIVED SO MANY DIFFERENT, fragmented lives that I could barely find the slightest link between them. My former life was infinitely far away. A vague recollection from that time occasionally surfaced, then vanished almost immediately. I was endlessly trying to piece myself together again. But apparently I was not going about it the right way. The cracks were still gaping.

I treated myself as best I could. Years of the talking cure. First with a psychoanalyst who saved my life. Who saw no problem with me refusing the drugs I was prescribed at the hospital. Who helped me when I decided to go to university, even with the wasted year after I passed my baccalaureate.

A miracle: thanks to a friend's intervention, who pleaded my cause with the head of my former school, I was accepted into the school's *classe préparatoire,* an intensive post-baccalaureate course of study for entry into the elite French universities. I can never thank both of them enough. I was back on my feet, though I felt like a blank page. Empty. No depth. I had a reputation. In order to fit in, to live a normal life, I put on a mask, concealed who I was, went to ground.

Two or three lives later, the same first name, last name, face, of course, but none of it mattered. Every two or three years I'd change my life completely. I'd find a new lover, new friends, a new job, a new way of dressing, a new hair color, a new way of speaking. I even changed countries.

Whenever anyone sounded me out about my past, a few flickering images would emerge from a thick fog, without ever consolidating. I wanted to leave no trace or impression. I had no nostalgia at all for my childhood or adolescence. I was floating above my own self, never where I should be. I didn't know who I was, or what I wanted. I let myself drift. I felt like I'd been alive for a thousand years.

I never spoke about my "first time."

"How old were you, who was it with?"

Ah, if only you knew.

I had a few close friends who'd been witness to that time of my life, but they rarely brought it up. The past was the past. We all have a history to overcome. Theirs had not always been straightforward either.

Since then, I have been with many men. Loving them wasn't hard. Trusting them was another story. Always on the defensive, I would ascribe intentions to them that they didn't necessarily have: that they wanted to use me, manipulate me, deceive me, that they cared only about themselves.

Whenever a man tried to give me pleasure, or worse still, tried to take his pleasure through me, I had to fight against a kind of disgust crouching in the shadows, about to swoop down on me, against a symbolic violence, which wasn't really there, that I imputed to every gesture.

It took me a long time to be able to sleep with a man without the aid of alcohol or psychotropic drugs. To be able, without any hidden agenda, to surrender myself, with my eyes closed, to another body. To find the path to my own desire.

It took me a long time, many years, to finally meet a man with whom I felt completely secure.

Part Six

WRITING

Language has always been an exclusive domain.
Who owns language owns power.

—Chloé Delaume, *My Beloved Sisters*

I WORKED A RANGE OF JOBS BEFORE I FOUND MYSELF caught up in the world of publishing. How wonderfully cunning the unconscious can be. It's impossible to escape its determinism. After having turned my back on books for many years, at last they were my friends again. Now I made my living through them. After all, books are what I know best.

I was trying, I suppose, feeling my way toward repairing something. But what? How? I put all my energy into texts written by other people. Unconsciously I was still trying to find some answers, a few sparse fragments of my history. I was hoping that in this way the mystery would somehow be resolved. What happened to "little V."? Has anyone seen her? Sometimes a voice used to arise from the depths and whisper in my ear:

"Books are lies." Now I no longer heard it, as if it had been wiped from my memory. Every now and then, a flash. A detail, here or there. I would think yes, that's it, that's a piece of me, between the lines, behind those words. I gathered them up. I collected them. I put myself together again. Books can be excellent medicine. I'd forgotten.

But every time I thought I was finally free, G. would find me again and try to renew his hold on me. Even when I became an adult, whenever someone mentioned his name to me, I would freeze, turn back into the adolescent I had been when I first met him. I'll be fourteen years old for the rest of my life. That was my fate.

One day my mother handed me one of the letters that, as he didn't know where I lived, he persisted in sending to her address. My silence, my refusal to communicate with him in any way, hadn't discouraged him at all. With astonishing nerve, he was writing to ask permission to publish photographs of me in a biography of him that one of his admirers was working on for a Belgian publisher. A lawyer friend of mine wrote him a threatening letter on my behalf. If G. persisted in any way in using my name or my image in the context of a literary work, legal action would be taken against him. G. did not pursue the project. At last I was safe. For now.

A few months later I discovered that G. had an official internet site that featured, in addition to a chronology of his life and work, photographs of some of his conquests, including two pictures of me at the age of fourteen, captioned with my initial, V., which encapsulated my identity from then on (to the point that I still sign my e-mails that way).

The shock was unbearable. I called my lawyer friend, who recommended a colleague more experienced than he in image copyright law. The affidavit we requested was expensive enough and, after lengthy research, my new adviser told me that unfortunately there was not much we could do. The site was registered not in G.'s name, but in that of a webmaster domiciled somewhere in Asia.

"G.M. has taken care of things so perfectly that he can't be deemed owner of the content hosted by his dummy corporation, which is completely outside French jurisdiction. Legally, the site is the work of a fan, nothing more. It's a totally cynical move, but it's absolutely airtight."

"How could a stranger living in Asia possibly have managed to get hold of photos of me at the age of fourteen? Photographs that belonged to G.? It doesn't add up."

"If you haven't got copies of the pictures, it will be hard to prove they're of you," she said, deeply apologetic. "By the way, I made some inquiries: G. has recently become the client of a leading light in intellectual property, one of the most redoubtable lawyers around. Getting into a legal battle with him would be a fool's errand. It could cost you not only your annual salary but also your health. Are you sure it's really worth it?"

With a heavy heart, I dropped the case.

IRONICALLY, I WAS NOW WORKING FOR THE PUBLISHER who had originally brought out G.'s notorious essay, *Under Sixteen*, in the 1960s.

Before taking the job, I checked that the rights to the book hadn't been renewed: this was indeed the case, though I didn't know why. I convinced myself that it was because of the publisher's moral disapproval. The reality was rather more prosaic: it was actually due to the growing scarcity of connoisseurs of this type of publication, or at least to the fact that increasingly they were too ashamed to admit to their predilection.

Unfortunately, G. continued to command respect at most of the Parisian publishing houses. And, more than thirty years after we first met, he couldn't stop himself from repeatedly verifying that he still had a hold on me. I don't know how he managed to find out where I was working, but the literary world is the size of a pocket handkerchief, and gossip was rife.

There was no point trying to work out how he'd discovered where I was working. One morning I got to my desk and found a long, embarrassed e-mail from my boss. G. had been pestering her for weeks, sending her messages begging her to act as an intermediary between him and me.

"I'm so sorry, V. I've been trying to keep him away from you for a while now so he can't bother you. But nothing seems to mollify him, so eventually I decided to talk to you and forward you his e-mails," she wrote.

In their e-mail exchange, which I read numb with shame, G. recounted our relationship in minute detail (just in case she was not aware of it, and as if it was any of her business). Not only was this an unbearable violation of my private life, but his tone was both ingratiating and pathetic. In an attempt to provoke her pity, he claimed, among other nonsense, that he was dying, and told her that his dearest desire was to see me again. He was suffering from a serious illness and would not be at peace bidding farewell to the world of the living without seeing my dear face one more time, blah, blah, blah . . . This was why he was beseeching her at all cost to forward me his messages. As if it went without saying that she was going to pander to his every whim.

Since he didn't have my home address, he went on to apologize for being reduced to writing to me at my workplace. He was utterly shameless. Disingenuously, he expressed surprise that I had not replied to the letter (in reality, there were many) that he had sent me not long ago, wondering if it might be because of the publisher's recent move to new offices.

The truth was, I had several times found letters from him on my desk, which I systematically threw in the bin without reading. Once, to trick me into opening it, someone else, whose handwriting I didn't recognize, had written my name and address on the envelope. It made no difference; the content had remained unchanged for thirty years: My continuing silence was a mystery. I must be consumed with regret at the thought of having destroyed such a noble union, not to mention having made him suffer so! He would never forgive me for having left him. He had nothing to apologize for. I was the guilty party, guilty of having brought to an end the most beautiful love story ever lived by a man and a teenage girl. Whatever I said, I belonged to him and I always would because, thanks to his books, our wild passion would never cease to light up the night.

In G.'s response to the point-blank refusal of the publishing director with whom I worked to intercede on his behalf, one sentence in particular leapt out at me: "No, I will never be relegated to V.'s past, nor she to mine."

Once again, I was filled with blind rage, fury, and powerlessness.

He was never going to leave me in peace.

Sitting in front of my computer screen, I burst into tears.

HAVING BEEN LARGELY COLD-SHOULDERED FOR A COUPLE of decades, G. made a triumphant return to the literary scene in 2013 when he was awarded the prestigious Prix Renaudot for his most recent book-length essay. People I respected were eager to appear on television to acclaim publicly the indisputable talent of this major literary figure. So be it. That wasn't really the issue. My own personal experience prevented me from objectively being able to judge his work, which repulsed me. In terms of its significance, however, I would have preferred the reserve that had been increasingly expressed over the previous twenty years, in terms of both the way he carried on in his private life and the ideas he espoused in some of his books, to continue, and to go further.

There was a disappointingly low-key controversy when the prize was awarded. A few journalists (young, for the most part, of neither his generation nor mine) spoke out against him being awarded this honorary distinction. G., meanwhile, in the speech he gave at the prize-giving ceremony, assumed that the prize was not for one book, but for the whole of his oeuvre, though this was not the case.

"To judge a book, a painting, a sculpture, or a film, not for its beauty, or the power of its expression, but for its morality or supposed immorality, is a spectacularly stupid thing to do; but on top of that, to promote the toxic idea of writing or signing a petition as a way of expressing outrage at the positive reception that people of taste have given the work—a petition whose sole purpose is to cause pain to the writer, painter, sculptor, or filmmaker—is simply despicable," he protested in a newspaper.

"Simply despicable"?

And going abroad to help yourself to some "young asses," paid for with the royalties you accumulated with descriptions of having sex with schoolgirls and publishing photographs of them on the internet without their consent and under the cover of anonymity—how would you describe that?

Today, I work in publishing, and I find it very hard to understand how some of the most renowned editors in the literary world could have published G.'s diaries, complete with first names, places, dates, and enough detail to make it possible at least for those who know them to identify his victims, without first having offered a minimum of hindsight in terms of the books' content. Particularly when it is explicitly stated on the cover that this is the text of the author's diary and not a work of fiction behind which he might cunningly have concealed himself.

I spent a long time thinking about this breach of confidentiality, particularly in a legal area that is otherwise strictly controlled, and I could only come up with one explanation. If it is illegal for an adult to have a sexual relationship with a minor who is under the age of fifteen, why is it tolerated when it is perpetrated by a representative of the artistic elite—a photographer, writer, filmmaker, or painter? It seems that an artist is of a separate caste, a being with superior virtues granted the ultimate authorization, in return for which he is required only to create an original and subversive piece of work. A sort of aristocrat in possession of exceptional privileges before whom we, in a state of blind stupefaction, suspend all judgment.

Were any other person to publish on social media a description of having sex with a child in the Philippines or brag about his collection of fourteen-year-old mistresses, he would find himself dealing with the police and be instantly considered a criminal.

Apart from artists, we have witnessed only Catholic priests being bestowed such a level of impunity.

Does literature really excuse everything?

ON TWO OCCASIONS I CROSSED PATHS WITH THE YOUNG woman whose name I had come across in G.'s famous little black book. Nathalie was one of G.'s many conquests during our affair, which he always strenuously denied.

The first time I saw her was in the brasserie where G. was a regular. A table was permanently reserved for him, and he had taken me to dinner there only a few months earlier. I went in to buy a packet of cigarettes late one evening, thinking it was unlikely that G. would be there, since he was very much not a night owl. Unfortunately, on this occasion I was mistaken. I spotted him immediately, sitting opposite a very young woman. I was troubled by her youth and radiance. I felt instantly old. I wasn't yet sixteen. I had ended the relationship almost a year earlier.

Five years later, I came out of a lecture at the Sorbonne and was walking down Boulevard Saint-Michel, when I heard a voice calling my name over and over from the opposite side of the street. I turned but didn't immediately recognize the young woman waving at me. She ran across the street and almost got herself knocked over, reminded me that her name was Nathalie, and, slightly embarrassed, mentioned the brief, upsetting glimpse we'd had of each other that evening in the smoky interior of a Parisian brasserie where G. had been vulgar enough to greet me with a triumphant smile. She asked me if I had time for a coffee. I wasn't sure I had any desire to talk to her about anything whatsoever, but something intrigued me; her face had lost the glow that had so upset me five years earlier and made me believe my youth had been stolen by hers. I suppose I might, narcissistically, have felt some satisfaction, savored the feeling of revenge. She had a hell of a cheek, stopping me like that in the middle of the street, when five years before she'd begun sleeping with G. while I was still in a relationship with him. But I could see she didn't look very well. Her face was gaunt with anxiety.

I smiled at her and agreed to a brief chat, despite her slightly rambling and agitated air. We sat down and her words began to spill out. Nathalie told me about her childhood, her broken family and absent father. How could I not recognize myself in her words? The same scenario. The same suffering. She told me how G. had hurt her, manipulated her in order to alienate her from her family and friends, from everything that makes up the life of a young woman. Then she reminded me of how G. made love, so mechanical and repetitive. Another poor little girl who had mistaken sex for love. I recognized everything she said, it all came back to me, every detail, and as the words poured out, I felt feverish, desperate to relate with the same precision how painful the memory of that experience remained for me.

Nathalie kept talking, apologizing, biting her lip, laughing nervously. If G. had witnessed our encounter, he would certainly have been horrified; he had always made sure that his mistresses never met, presumably for fear of seeing them turn into a furious horde hatching some joint revenge against him.

We both felt that we had broken a taboo. What was it that linked us, brought us together, deep down? An overwhelming need to confide in someone who would understand. It was a relief as well for me to find myself in solidarity with this girl, who had once been one of my many rivals.

In the solace conferred by our newfound sisterhood, we tried to comfort each other: this episode was well and truly behind us, and now we could even laugh about it, without jealousy, pain, or despair.

"To think he thought he was a champion, such a great lover, when in reality he was completely pathetic!"

We began to laugh hysterically. All of a sudden Nathalie's expression grew calm and radiant again. She looked like the young woman I had admired five years before.

Then we talked about the young boys, Manila.

"Do you think he's homosexual? Or an actual pedophile?" Nathalie asked.

"I'd say more an *ephebophile.*" (I'd studied literature, and had come across this word, which I was very proud of, when reading some author whose name I've forgotten.) "He's turned on by puberty, which is presumably the age he's stuck at himself. However brilliant he is, his psyche is that of an adolescent. And when he's with a young girl, he feels like a fourteen-year-old boy. That's the reason he doesn't think he's doing anything wrong."

Nathalie burst out laughing again.

"You're right! I prefer to think of him like that. I feel so dirty sometimes. As if I was the one who'd been sleeping with eleven-year-old boys in the Philippines."

"No, it's not you, Nathalie, it's not our fault. We're like those boys: we had no one to protect us then, we felt like he made us exist, even though he was just using us. Maybe he didn't even mean to; it's just his pathology."

"At least we can sleep with whoever we like now, not just old men!" Nathalie giggled.

I had proof now: I wasn't the only one carrying the burden of my relationship with G. And, contrary to what he recounted in his books, he did not leave his young mistresses with nothing but warm memories.

We didn't exchange phone numbers or anything that would have allowed us to see each other again one day. We had no reason to. We embraced, holding each other tight, and wished each other well.

What became of Nathalie? I hope she met a boy her own age who loved her along with her suffering, who helped rid her of her shame. I hope she won that fight. But how many other girls are out there, clinging to the shadows, their faces, like hers that day, gaunt with defeat, desperate for someone to listen to them?

IT'S INCREDIBLE. I'D NEVER HAVE BELIEVED IT POSSIBLE. After so many romantic disasters, such a struggle to accept love unhesitatingly, the man whom I eventually met and with whom I now share my life was somehow able to heal my many wounds. We have a son who is just entering adolescence. A son who has helped me grow. Because you can't remain fourteen years old forever once you become a mother. My son is handsome, with a gentle expression in his eyes, a bit of a dreamer. Fortunately, he never asks me much about my childhood. Which is just as well. In the imaginations of our children, at least when they're young, our lives only began with their birth. Perhaps they sense, intuitively, that there is a shadowy zone it's better not to venture into.

Whenever I go through a period of depression or suffer an uncontrollable panic attack, I tend to take it out on my mother. Pathologically, I am constantly trying to force an apology from her, or at least an iota of contrition. But no matter how much I berate her, she not only never concedes; she digs her heels in even more. Whenever I try to make her change her mind by pointing out all the young teenagers around us—"Can't you see, a fourteen-year-old girl is still a kid?"—she replies, "That's irrelevant. You were much more mature at the same age."

And then, the day I asked her to read the manuscript of this book, dreading her reaction more than anyone else's, she wrote back: "Don't change a thing. This is your story."

Now G. has reached the venerable age of eighty-three. As far as our relationship is concerned, the statute of limitations has long passed and the moment has come when—blessed be the passage of time—his fame has finally dimmed, and his most transgressive books have sunk into oblivion.

Many long years passed before I decided to write this book, and even more before I could bear to see it published. I wasn't ready until now. The obstacles appeared insurmountable. First there was the fear of the consequences such a detailed account of this episode would have on my family and my career, which are always difficult to evaluate.

I also had to overcome my fear of the tiny circle of friends who might still be prepared to protect G. This was not trivial. I was worried that if the book were published, I'd be subject to violent attacks not only by his fans but also by some ex-*soixante-huitards*, veterans of the May '68 revolution, who might feel they were being attacked for having signed his notorious open letter; and perhaps even a few women opposed to the new so-called neo-Puritan discourse on sexuality; in other words, all the self-appointed critics of the policing of public morals.

To give myself courage, I clung to this argument: if I wanted to assuage my fury once and for all, and reclaim this chapter of my life, writing was without doubt the best way to do it. Over the years a few people have suggested the idea. Others, meanwhile, in my own interest, have tried to dissuade me.

It was the man I love who finally persuaded me that writing meant becoming once more the subject of my own story. A story that had been denied me for too long.

To tell the truth, I am surprised that someone else, some other young girl from that time, hasn't already written her own book in an attempt to correct the interminable succession of marvelous sexual initiations that G. describes in his books. I'd have loved someone else to do it instead of me. Someone more gifted, cleverer, more impartial too. It would certainly have unburdened me of a great weight. The silence apparently corroborates what G. has always claimed, offering proof that no teenage girl has ever had reason to complain of having been in a relationship with him.

I don't think that's really the case. I believe that it is extremely difficult to extricate oneself from someone's hold, even ten, twenty, thirty years later. It is hard to shake the feeling of self-doubt, the sense of being complicit in a love that one felt oneself, in the attraction that we once aroused in him; this is what has held us back, even more than the few fans G. still has in the Parisian literary world.

By setting his sights on young, lonely, vulnerable girls, whose parents either couldn't cope or were actively negligent, G. knew that they would never threaten his reputation. And silence means consent.

But on the other hand, to my knowledge, not a single one of his countless mistresses has ever chosen to write a book recounting the wonderful relationship she had with G.

Does that tell us something?

What has changed today—something that men like he and his defenders complain about constantly, excoriating the general atmosphere of puritanism—is that following the sexual revolution, it is now, at last, the turn of the victims to speak out.

NOT LONG AGO, I WAS CONTEMPLATING A VISIT TO THE renowned Institute for Contemporary Publishing Archives. There, in a magnificently renovated former abbey just outside of Caen, visitors may make an appointment to consult, among other treasures, the original manuscripts of Marcel Proust and Marguerite Duras. Before going, I searched the internet for a list of the authors whose archives are preserved there, and, to my astonishment, there was the name of G.M. A few months previously he had donated to this noble institution all his manuscripts, including the correspondence from his love affairs. At last, his posterity is guaranteed. His works are now a part of literary history.

For the time being, I have decided not to visit the Institute. I picture myself sitting down in the grand reading room in solemn silence to decipher the spidery handwriting of one of my favorite authors, all the while wondering if the person sitting next to me is consulting the letters I wrote when I was fourteen. I imagine myself applying for permission to access these letters. I'd have to invent some untruth, a thesis on transgression in the fiction of the second half of the twentieth century, a dissertation on the collected works of G.M. Would my request have to be submitted to him first? Would his authorization be required? What an irony, to be obliged to employ such a ruse for the right to read my own letters.

In the meantime, and although the thought of book burning has always filled me with horror, I wouldn't be opposed to a great carnival of confetti made from my signed books and all the letters from G. I found recently at the bottom of a box left at my mother's apartment for all these years. I'll spread them out around me, and with a big pair of scissors I'll snip them carefully into tiny bits of paper that I'll throw in the air on a windy day in some secret corner of the Luxembourg Gardens.

At least posterity won't have them then.

Postscript

Warning to the reader

Between the lines, and sometimes in the most direct and crude way, some of G.M.'s books constitute an explicit apology for child sexual abuse. Literature considers itself to be above moral judgment, but it is our responsibility as publishers to keep in mind that a sexual relationship between an adult and a minor is a culpable act, punishable by law.

See, it can't be that hard if even I can write those words.

Acknowledgments

My thanks go to Claire Le Ho-Devianne, the first "objective" reader of this book, for her comments and encouragement.

My thanks also to Olivier Nora, who agreed without hesitation to publish it, for his faith and loyalty.

And finally, thanks to Juliette Joste for her sensitive editing and her unwavering support.

A Note from the Translator

When I first read *Le Consentement*, some time before the opportunity to translate it came my way, I shivered at the portrayal of the claustrophobic world of St. Germain des Prés that Vanessa Springora conjures with such deft precision. It's a tiny area of Paris, but the power it exerts as the nexus of generations of literary dreams and fantasies remains strong in the minds of Parisians and visitors alike. Springora was born into this quasi-aristocratic world and knows it intimately. Her ability to evoke its intricate social codes and superficial glamour, the painfully gendered hierarchies of social, literary, and political entitlement, infuses the book with nervy, mercurial intensity.

The challenge for the translator is to navigate the multiple registers of the prose, to match the nimble, suggestive descriptions of social occasions and interpersonal dramas, so brilliantly summoned in French, sometimes in barely more than a single word or phrase. Most important of all, the translator must summon with the same nuance the double vision that characterizes the narrative: the child's view of the world as it segues into that of the adult looking back. Springora's taut fury as she recounts her experiences of her abuse and subsequent breakdown is modified by her benevolent pity for her younger self, a "broken toy" who has had to struggle so hard to learn to trust and love again.

Consent is a memoir of abuse, but it is also a penetrating exploration of both language and literature—specifically French—as a vector of power. Springora's abuser, "G.M.," a self-styled "great writer," is horrified at the thought of anyone abusing his beloved French, while unashamedly indulging in the grotesque sexual and emotional abuse of children. He lays romantic store in the notion that his elegant way with prose will save him, not from himself, or the wrath of God, but from the grimly bourgeois straitjacket of conventional morality, and, more prosaically, from jail. Springora wonders, as many others have, why such behavior is tolerated "when it is perpetrated by a representative of the artistic elite—a photographer, writer, filmmaker, or painter. It seems that an artist is of a separate caste, a being with superior virtues granted the ultimate authorization, in return for which he is required only to create an original and subversive piece of work. A sort of aristocrat in possession of exceptional privileges before whom we, in a state of blind stupefaction, suspend all judgment."

Even at the age of fourteen, Springora instinctively understands that her abuser is using language to steal her soul. One day he determines to write her assignment for school, an experience she describes as a "dispossession." Throughout their relationship he takes endless notes in his Moleskine notebooks, and uses them later to turn her, barely disguised, into a character in several novels that are published to some acclaim by the most esteemed Parisian publishing houses. "I was just a character, living on borrowed time, like every other girl who'd come before me. It wouldn't be long before he erased me completely from the pages of his wretched diary. For his readers, it was merely a story, words." The money he earns from his writing finances his trips to the Philippines where he further indulges his pedophilia, tales of which then fill his published diaries. He carries a letter from President Mitterrand around with him wherever he goes, like a talisman, convinced that the president's mellifluous praise will keep him from arrest.

It is only after several years that Springora returns, with some reluctance, to the world of publishing and literature she has turned her back on for so long. Having been tormented for years by the annual publication of a novel or collection of letters that feature her or her correspondence with G.M., having been "trapped in a deceptive likeness, a reductive version of [myself], a grotesque, contorted snapshot," she finds herself restored, mended, able to live and love in a way that for so long she believed she would never be able to. She realizes, triumphantly, that the same language that had once exerted its insidious power over her was now to be the instrument of her salvation, enabling her not only to name and shame G.M. himself, but to extend her criticism to all those both in publishing and in the Parisian intellectual world in general who protected and supported him for so many years. If she has learned one thing from her abuser it is what every writer and translator knows: that there is no such thing as "merely a story," or "merely words." She finally understands that the only way to become the subject of her own story is to write it down: "Why not ensnare the hunter in his own trap, ambush him within the pages of a book?"

Natasha Lehrer
Paris, August 2020

Here ends Vanessa Springora's

Consent.

The first edition of this book was printed and bound at at LSC Communications in Harrisonburg, Virginia, February 2021.

A NOTE ON THE TYPE

The text of this novel was set in Dante, a typeface first developed by German-Italian printer and type designer Giovanni Mardersteig (1892–1977), founder of private press Officina Bodoni. Officina Bodoni quickly gained a reputation for their high-quality printing, and Mardesteig approached typefaces with the same perfectionism. Dante was released for mechanical composition in 1957. The digital version, which you see on this page, was redrawn by Monotype's Ron Carpenter and released in 1993. Based in part on Luca Pacioli's renaissance face, Dante is an exquisite, balanced serif font, making it perfect for print.

An imprint dedicated to publishing international voices, offering readers a chance to encounter other lives and other points of view via the language of the imagination.

www.ingramcontent.com/pod-product-compliance
Lightning Source LLC
Chambersburg PA
CBHW021601130726
48086CB00027B/595

* 9 7 8 0 0 6 3 0 4 7 9 0 7 *